Praise for *Things I Wish I'd Known*

'This collection of very funny essays is the essential gift for pregnant friends.' *Stylist*

'Step away from the airy-fairy earth mother accounts of the miracle of birth and cackle along with these more realistic recollections.' *Grazia*

'A collection of funny, inspirational and brutally honest accounts of becoming a mother.' *Hello!*

'From labour and IVF to weaning and post-birth sex, each author is brutally honest about their experiences, ensuring you will laugh and cry along with them.' *Essentials*

'Like a hilarious series of conversations with your non-judgmental girlfriends. Honest and refreshing, and it made me feel like I'm not alone as I try to navigate life as a new mum.' *The Advocate*

'A very funny, yet moving collection that will resonate with all mums.' *Made for Mums*

'Filled to the brim with the type of parenting advice you wish your friends had actually told you.' *Pregnancy & Parenting*

‘Witty and honest accounts of motherhood.’ *Sainsbury’s Magazine*

‘Sometimes funny, sometimes sad, and always genuine.’
Angels & Urchins

‘Whether you want to prepare for future motherhood or reminisce fondly, we know just the book for you.’
Woman & Home

THINGS I wish I'd Known

WOMEN TELL THE TRUTH ABOUT MOTHERHOOD

EDITED BY VICTORIA YOUNG

Foreword by Justine Roberts

Contributors:

Adele Parks, Kathy Lette, Cathy Kelly, Bryony Gordon, Jenny Colgan, Christina Hopkinson, Anne Marie Scanlon, Emma Freud, Tiffanie Darke, Anna Moore, Esther Walker, Rachel Johnson, Lucy Porter, Afsaneh Knight, Clover Stroud, Nicci Gerard, Daisy Garnett, Alix Walker, Shobna Gulati

ICON

This edition published in the UK in 2016 by
Icon Books Ltd, Omnibus Business Centre,
39–41 North Road, London N7 9DP
email: info@iconbooks.com
www.iconbooks.com

First published in the UK in 2015 by Icon Books Ltd

Sold in the UK, Europe and Asia
by Faber & Faber Ltd, Bloomsbury House,
74–77 Great Russell Street,
London WC1B 3DA or their agents

Distributed in the UK, Europe and Asia
by TBS Ltd, TBS Distribution Centre, Colchester Road,
Frating Green, Colchester CO7 7DW

Distributed in Australia and New Zealand
by Allen & Unwin Pty Ltd,
PO Box 8500, 83 Alexander Street,
Crows Nest, NSW 2065

Distributed in South Africa by
Jonathan Ball, Office B4, The District,
41 Sir Lowry Road, Woodstock 7925

ISBN: 978-178578-037-0

Typeset in ITC Esprit by Marie Doherty

Printed and bound in the UK by Clays Ltd, St Ives plc

For Tom and Max

Victoria Young is a journalist and magazine editor. She started her career in New York where she worked at *The New York Times*, then returned to London to work at *YOU* magazine, *Red* magazine and the *Evening Standard*, and has written for many other publications. Most recently she was Assistant Editor of *Woman & Home* magazine. Victoria lives with her husband and son in East London.

Contents

Introduction

By Victoria Young

This is the book I wish had existed during my first few years of motherhood. If you've picked it up and are wondering whether it's for you, or maybe for someone you know, the first thing to mention is that this is definitely not a 'How To' book. Rather, what you will find here is a collection of very different women sharing their unique, honest experience of motherhood: the highs and the lows, the funny bits and the sad bits, the good, the bad – and the not always pretty.

When I first started approaching women asking them if they wanted to write something about motherhood, the overwhelming response was 'yes' – they all had so much to say. But what really struck me as the book started coming together is that every single woman wanted to write about something different, whether it was navigating the world as a single mother of an unplanned baby, having a baby who thought sleep was for losers or how to nurture a relationship that has gone from being two to three. And that's the thing about motherhood – there are as many ways to be a mother as there are women, and there is no one right way to do any of it. It's just that when you are surrounded by all those 'how-to' books it's easy to get confused and think that they are right, and you are wrong.

When I was first pregnant, four years ago, I spent

hour upon endless hour thinking about my pregnancy and birth: buying a birthing pool, reading books about natural birth and assembling an ambient playlist in preparation for my home birth. But I gave barely any thought to what would happen if things didn't quite pan out as I'd planned (like, say, if my home birth ended up being an emergency C-section). And although I was aware, in the most abstract way, that life as I knew it was about to change, the amount of time I spent dwelling on what life would actually be like once the baby had arrived was virtually nil. Or, rather, the time I spent thinking about it was coloured by, for example, my NCT class on breastfeeding, which consisted mainly of describing how, left to its own devices, my newborn would crawl up my tummy and 'self-latch'.

In my case that information turned out to be so inaccurate as to be almost criminal, and, in retrospect, I wish I had asked for my money back. Unfortunately, I was too busy sitting on the sofa with each boob tethered to a milk-expressing flagon to do much of anything else for six months, because no matter how hard I tried – and BOY, did I try – breastfeeding didn't really happen. But I really hung on in there with the expressing because at that stage I was still certain that denying your child breast milk was tantamount to child abuse, and that formula is the devil, obviously.* I know lots of women take happily to breastfeeding like

* My revised view, for what it is worth, is that formula really is NOT the devil. If you are having a hard time breastfeeding, please, please just give your baby a bottle of formula and give yourself a break.

ducks to water, and that is a wonderful thing. I just wish I'd prepared for the possibility that not everyone does. The bottom line is that, despite reading many manuals about the theory of motherhood, somehow none of them even remotely prepared me for the reality of it.

The propaganda about motherhood starts in pregnancy, when people cross crowded rooms to stroke your bump and tell you, misty-eyed, how much they miss those early days and what a wonderful mother you will be. It's lovely, in a way, how society conspires to treat pregnant women like fragile creatures who will be transported on a cloud to the flower-scented meadow of motherhood. But it's not very helpful. For some reason it's deemed cruel or distasteful or unfair to talk honestly to pregnant women about what lies ahead. Instead, people – and weirdly, it's mostly other women – perpetuate a vague, fluffy idealisation of the truth that can be projected and spun out for nine months, which pregnant women, who know no better, get lulled into believing.

The problem with that, of course, is that when the baby actually comes along, the reality can be that much harder to deal with. Worse, it can leave women feeling they must be somehow lacking as a mother if they find it difficult. I know I felt that way. Even so, somehow the realities of motherhood often remain a hidden world, not talked about out loud.

But what I have slowly discovered is that everyone has a different experience and, often, it's not straightforward. For every woman who has had an ecstatic birth followed by unparalleled joy and happiness at being a mother, there is someone for whom parenthood has had a difficult start because of colic (unexplained and relentless crying), a sleepless baby or because they are doing it solo – or just because of bewilderment at this new state of affairs: adjusting to having a third person in your relationship or to having a body that is battle-scarred and unrecognisable. Not to mention never having even close to enough sleep.

Personally, I probably had an unusually difficult start to motherhood – my baby was hospitalised for a week when he was ten days old because he was so dehydrated, after which he was tube-fed (and had nothing by mouth) for twelve weeks while doctors decided whether there was something wrong with his swallow. As it turned out there was not, but by the time the feeding tube came out, my son had lost the urge to breastfeed. So that was tough,* and not at all what I'd expected those early days to be like.

But I found other aspects hard too. After paternity leave ended, my husband – with whom I had shared an equal partnership until that point – disappeared off to work every day while I stayed at home bouncing on my birthing ball to soothe the baby, then expressing milk, then feeding. Bouncing, pumping, feeding. Bouncing, pumping, feeding. There I sat, bouncing, all day, thinking: 'Where has my life gone?' and feeling a bit guilty that I wasn't having the time of my life, as advertised throughout the duration of my pregnancy.

---

* Understatement!

But when I mentioned I was finding it hard to anyone who asked how I was doing, I realised that was the wrong answer. Bizarrely, when you are learning how to do the most challenging new job you'll probably ever do, you're under pressure to pretend that everything's going brilliantly.

Looking back, I wish I had been able to read more about other people's actual experiences of motherhood, rather than how it 'should' be. Instead of reading manuals about what to do, I wish I'd read more about the myriad ways that things – from the birth to sleeping, to weaning, to toddlers, to teenagers and everything in between – actually do pan out. After all, there is nothing like knowing you are not alone.

The feeding thing turned out to be my big hurdle. Once we got that sorted, everything slowly started to get easier. Gradually, the angst subsided, I found my feet and I started to really enjoy it. Of course, there will be more challenges ahead, but now I am the mother of a funny, sweet and very loving little boy who has slowly lit up my world and filled it with more joy, fun and love than I had ever hoped I'd be allocated in life – and having a child is by far the best thing I have ever done.

If I could go back in time to talk to myself as I sat beflagoned and bewildered on the sofa, then I would probably say something along the lines of: 'Don't panic. Yes, your life feels like it has disappeared overnight, but it will come back – with bells on. Oh, he will eat like a trooper. And it doesn't matter whether he breastfeeds or not.

At some point he'll start sleeping through the night. You'll get the hang of it – really you will. He's amazing. Nothing much else matters. All will be well. And you are doing a brilliant job.'

I very much hope this book will do something similar for you. Whether you are a seasoned mother or father, or just recently swept away on the tidal wave that is new parenthood, the aim is to offer some humour, hope and perspective. If nothing else, I hope you will take heart that you are not alone. But I hope the main thing this book makes you realise is that no one can do a better job than you.

Foreword

By Justine Roberts, co-founder of Mumsnet

In spite of having spent thirteen-plus years now being a parent and around twelve of those years running a parenting website, and in spite of having spent a fair bit of that time thinking about what it means to be a mother (when I wasn't thinking about head lice, maths homework, search engine optimisation or poo), I still feel like you could fit my conclusions about this whole motherhood malarkey on the back of an envelope. And if you weeded out the bits that sound like the sappier type of Mother's Day card, my words of wisdom would probably fit nicely on a postage stamp. And of course I have frequent days when my thirteen-year-old daughters send me letters detailing my many and various parenting sins … and usually they've got a point.

However, one thing I can say that hanging out on a website for mothers and reading their thousands of differing views has taught me is that there is no standard template for a good and effective mother. Among our regular users, there are some impressive teen mothers, a fair few who have had one or more children in their mid-forties, some inspiring mothers of children with special needs, a lot of full-time working mothers and full-time stay-at-home mothers, mothers of seven and mothers of one, single mothers, lesbian mothers, stepmothers and adoptive mothers. There are amazing mothers who cope with their own physical disabilities or mental illnesses. There are some who grind up carrots, others who get out jars and some who hand their babies a carrot baton. Women who do the school run in stilettos and a full face of slap and others who cruise through the day in their PJs. And the great thing about a website like Mumsnet is that often you don't actually know any of these things about a person when they first start posting – so you only later find out that the fantastic advice about helping a child with school anxiety came to you courtesy of a mother still struggling with PND (or a dad). The internet is a great leveller, and it hits you when your prejudices are down. That anonymity can be a liberating thing, because while there may be many more ways to choose to be a mother now, it also feels like there is far more scrutiny of mothers and what they do. And maybe we all need to learn to put away stereotypes and take off what Mumsnetters would call our 'judgey pants'.

As reproductive choices proliferate, it begins to seem that whatever choice we make (and how many of us have many real choices?) leaves us open to criticism. Having a child at all is selfish and ecologically irresponsible. Having a child too young is economically irresponsible. Having one too old is biologically irresponsible. And choosing not to have children is selfish and unnatural – the woman who decides not to be a mother often gets the worst press of all.

How and whether we choose to have children is only the first of many things for which mothers are held up to scrutiny. For women in the public eye, the relentless appraisal of body shape and size reaches new intensity during pregnancy and after childbirth. And you can't get it right – the mother who gets her figure back within six weeks of the birth is clearly not spending enough time with her baby. The actress mother who looks flabby and tired at an awards ceremony is the subject of gleeful tabloid *schadenfreude*. That scrutiny filters down to the rest of us and how we feel about our postnatal bodies. And that's just the beginning. It sometimes seems like barely a week goes by without the press reporting a new study about how some aspect of the way we look after our children – feeding, education, childcare – is fundamentally wrong and damaging. And a few months later another study demonstrates the opposite of the first study …

The fact that the most popular forum on Mumsnet is called 'Am I being unreasonable?' says much about the relentless self-analysis and need for validation that can go with the mothering territory. And truth be told, as well as a hell of a lot of advice and support and sharing of jokes, there is often a fair bit of judging that we're all guilty of from time to time – of a mother on the bus whose eighteen-month-old is downing a bottle of Coke or feeding himself from a jar of baby food, or of toddlers let out in cold weather without hats. Yet at the heart of Mumsnet is a core philosophy which boils down to this: 'There's more than one way to skin a cat.' And that's just what this book proves.

Lost Property

By Adele Parks

Adele Parks is a bestselling author who has written fourteen novels, the latest of which is *Spare Brides*. She lives in London with her husband, Jim, and son, Conrad, who is thirteen years old.

The hardest thing I had to come to terms with when I had my son was that I suddenly became public property. I was no longer an independent woman; I was defined through someone else. I was not 'Adele'; I was 'a mother'. It's funny, but marriage hadn't clipped my wings in any noticeable way; we were a young, reasonably affluent London couple who still pretty much did what we liked when we liked, and I certainly wasn't defined by myself or anyone else as 'a wife'. However, the moment I became a mum – in fact as soon as I was pregnant – I suddenly transformed into a being that every member of society seemed to have a view on, worse still, a view they were all too willing to share.

I was shocked by the degree to which other people would offer up unsolicited opinions as to how I should raise my child. I remember giving my son a bottle of milk in a supermarket café (I know, hold the glamour!). As it happened, it was actually breast milk that I had expressed (because I didn't always feel comfortable feeding in public), but a man in his forties came up to me and gave me a lecture about how breast was best and proceeded to tell me all the benefits I already was fully aware of. In effect, he was saying I was a bad mum for feeding in a way he disagreed with. This man didn't know if I had mastitis or a child who hadn't taken to the breast, or if I had simply decided to bottle-feed because, erm, it's *my* baby. I didn't bother to tell him it was breast milk, not because I didn't feel I had to justify myself (I did feel that, I still do, that's why I mention it now!). I just couldn't justify myself because I was too angry. I simply told him if he ever had to get his boobs out in public to be a parent then he could have a view, but until then he couldn't. He stormed off, outraged at my behaviour. OK, this wasn't necessarily a moment I'm particularly proud of, but I think you'll understand.

If the general public had confined their unsolicited advice to the parameters of how I should bring up my child, I might have managed to grin and bear it, to write off the interference as well-intentioned advice. However, it seemed to me that once I became a mum not only did everyone feel they could tell me how to do that exactly, but that they could pass comment on every aspect of my behaviour. Suddenly what I drank, ate, wore and said was scrutinised and judged. Received wisdom would have it that 'Good Mums' don't drink, they eat well, they shouldn't have time to look glamorous and they most certainly shouldn't say 'tits' out loud in a supermarket.

Views from family members are to be expected and to some extent tolerated; families do involve themselves in one another's lives, that's their job. But *everyone* has a view about how I ought to look after my baby: other parents, people without children, strangers in the street, journalists, shopkeepers, butchers, bakers, candlestick makers! Furthermore, the public aren't often that nice about mothers as a breed. It seemed to me that the word 'mum' was only ever attached to negative adjectives: 'Pushy Mum', 'Overprotective Mum', 'Slummy Mummy', 'Frumpy Mum'. It seemed it was a lot easier to get it wrong than to get it right.

There is a strong consensus (too strong for me to dare ignore) that new mothers must 'socialise' their babies, the accepted meaning of which is to take them to pre-arranged (often expensive) playgroups. This naturally means that mothers have to spend time with other people they may not have all that much in common with – other than possession of a small baby – all of whom have opinions that they are keen to share. Quickly new motherhood can begin to feel like a competition. If Freddie is sleeping through the night and Millie isn't, then the implication is that Millie's mum is doing something wrong. If Azma manages to get out of nappies before Zac, then Zac's mother is certainly to blame. Mums feel like failures on two counts: one) their child's development is perceived to be behind that of other children; and two) it has to be her fault! The question 'Does he eat avocados?' suddenly seems like a judgement, not just a rather yuppie comment on my son's digestive habits.

It's only in hindsight that I can see that questions from other mothers about my son's eating/sleeping/weeing/regurgitating habits were often more about insecurity than boastfulness. If only I'd known that at the time! Personally, I was plagued with a sense of 'Do they [other mothers] know something I don't?' It was illogical then that I didn't want them to tell me if they did! This is perhaps because of the inherited notion that women should all somehow instinctively know how to be mothers – no one wants to admit that their instincts might not be up to it.

As a new mother I had to come to terms with being public property – neighbours I'd never spoken to knocked on the door to get involved in my life, I had to join groups (I'm not a joiner, I'm actually quite a private person) and I had to answer to nursery teachers, midwives and health workers. I see the sense of these structures in our society and enormously respect the work done by these individuals, but I just hadn't expected them to be there in my life. I'd had a vision that it would be just me, my husband and our baby. Naive, I know. I felt extremely connected with my baby and I adored him, but I was not always comfortable with the new people who entered my life. I sometimes found them to be a distraction from the real business of mothering. (The infernal, endless coffee mornings one is supposed to attend!) I found it really peculiar that I was plunged into society in this way. For a time I resented it enormously but, as time went on, something altered; I started to value it. Eventually I came to understand that these groups (organised or organic) which spring up in our society are there to support a mother. I changed. We do, however much we think we won't.

My identity shifted. I'm pleased to report that I did not start wearing high-waisted jeans, bob my hair and suddenly find conversations about the texture of baby poo fascinating; I didn't! However, I did start to understand the value of hanging around with other women who might know the Ofsted reports on the local nurseries and who would forgive me for not having the energy finish a sentence. Slowly I got to a place where I didn't automatically dismiss or resent uninvited advice. Instead I sifted through it and often found invaluable nuggets of gold.

It took a lot of courage and reserve not to fall into any of the stereotypes of how the public imagine a mum ought to dress or what her interests are supposed to be. I made an effort to find the sort of women who celebrated the days I did have enough energy to put on lipstick and who gave me a high five if I managed to get my highlights done, rather than a disapproving glare. They are out there! I accepted that 99 per cent of the time the advice and information is well-intentioned, and the giver of the advice is just that – a giver. It was up to me to be adult enough to receive or reject it, but being resentful wasn't helpful or sensible. I wasted a lot of time being too proud to accept help and assuming interference was a criticism, rather than a genuine desire to help, to be humane and human. Over time I felt increasingly integrated with society. Before I had a baby I believe I was lost property, and then I became public property. I wish I'd known that isn't a bad thing.

THINGS I wish I'd Known

1 My baby threw up a lot. (Actually he probably threw up the normal amount, but he certainly threw up more than an adult, which was my yardstick up until becoming a mum!) I changed his entire outfit after every sick-up, which was exhausting and unnecessary. I wish I'd known then that the world doesn't stop if your baby has puke on his romper.

2 Ditto, your shoulder.

3 Competitive mothers are insecure. They are! If they have the time or need to compare your mothering skills with their own, or worse still, your baby with theirs, it's because they are unsure, not because they are mean. Still, it doesn't mean you have to hang around with them.

4 You don't need to be a martyr to motherhood. I was. It's probably not healthy.

5 It's OK to admit you are knackered, confused, fed up or all three.

6 It's OK to think your baby is the cleverest, prettiest, most alert baby ever, but only say as much to your partner and your mum. No one else agrees; if they pretend to agree then they are lovely friends, and you should hang on to them.

7 I wish I'd realised that my mother meant well when she was offering advice. She thinks I'm brilliant (I'm not, but see point six), and so she thinks she's done a great job. She also thinks I'm doing a great job being a mum; she was not trying to frustrate me.

8 It goes on and on; motherhood is not just about being a mum to a newborn. You have lots of time to get it right, make some mistakes and then get it right again. My 'baby' is thirteen at the time of writing …

9 I wish I'd taken photos every single day because it flies past and I would have liked to catch and bottle up as much as I could.

10 Everything is going to be OK.

11 After having children you don't just become a mother, you turn into your mother, too.

Lessons from Motherhood

By Daisy Garnett

Daisy Garnett lives in London with her husband, Nicholas, and their children, Rose, four, and Charlie Ray, two. She is a writer, freelance journalist and co-founder and editor of style and culture website A-Littlebird.com.

It's hard for me to pinpoint when I became a mother. The timing is complicated for reasons I'll explain, but I do remember precisely the moment I turned into the mother I didn't want to be. It was the day my daughter, then two years old, called me a 'silly bitch'. It came after a series of tantrums, a great many tears, a lot of hand-wringing, shouting and door-slamming, but it was delivered calmly and definitely along with this message: 'This time, today, I have won.'

And she had, the silly bitch. 'That's the thing,' a friend said to me when I asked him about his daughter, who was a year older than mine and always seemed impeccably behaved. He'd never raised his voice, ever, this parent, a father who worked long hours, and so wasn't with his children day in and day out. 'If you start shouting and behaving like them,' he explained, 'then they've won.' They have, I agreed. Mine had.

I gave birth to my first child, a beautiful son, on the day he was due, which was 12 January 2009. He was perfect – isn't every baby? – but, alas, he wasn't alive. I was told that his heart wasn't beating as I went into labour, which then proceeded, naturally, for twelve hours. When I was told that labour would continue I was amazed. I assumed that if your baby had died, then everything would stop, but no, you are told this news and then bam, another contraction arrives and then bam, another and then another, and you still feel your baby ripping through your body, so it's hard to believe that anything has ended. How can his heart have stopped, I thought, when he's pushing hard to get out into the world?

And so, at 3.12am on that January day, I became a mother, and for another twelve hours I held and cuddled and cradled my baby and stared into his tiny face and held his little hand and passed him over to his dad, so I could admire the two of them together, just like every other new mum does. Certainly, I had become a mother. Surely that was irrefutable? I had the stitches and the milk leaking out of my breasts and the still-pregnant-looking tummy. But I had to leave my baby in hospital, never to see him again, so I was also childless, which technically made me not a mother at all.

Rose arrived fourteen months later in March 2010 after a troubled pregnancy (entirely unrelated to Pip's death), which saw me spending part of Christmas Eve and Christmas Day in hospital to receive steroid injections to lessen the risk of her dying should she be born dangerously prematurely, as was predicted. In fact, she arrived only three weeks early, and we left the hospital a couple of hours after she was born to become parents, proper.

For the first two years everything was great. The first three months were tough because Rose had colic and cried for several hours every afternoon and into the evening, as colicky babies do, but it was also an insanely joyful time, and once the colic stopped it was as if the sun came out. She was a clingy baby, it turned out, though I barely noticed it, and what baby isn't? But, yes, I knew that the fact that she used my finger instead of a security blanket to stroke her top lip – her way (via me) of soothing herself – was just one indication that she was needier than many. One fellow mother, who I got to know in the park, laughed as she watched us and said, 'All Rose wants to do is get back into your tummy,' and her comment rang true. Sometimes it was maddening that she wouldn't let anyone else pick her up, including even her dad for a time, and of course it's a vicious circle: baby insists on mama, baby gets mama, so baby gets used to always having mama, and therefore only wants what she is used to (mama).

I know I was partly responsible for this; perhaps wholly so. She demanded me, so I gave her me. One friend told me that the intensity of my relationship with Rose was only to be expected after what had happened, a comment I took on board and both accepted – it was probably true – and somewhat resented. After all, I was still working. As a freelance journalist I could work from home while Rose played at my feet, when she napped and in the evenings. By the time she was six months old, she slept in her own bed, had been sleep-trained and began to be looked after by Ann, a brilliant childminder, for a few hours, twice a week. Her older half-sisters were also wonderful with her, often taking her for walks at weekends and in the holidays. So it wasn't as if I didn't let her out of my sight, even if I didn't know how to turn the volume down in terms of the intensity of our relationship when we were together, which was still most of the time.

It's true that I had changed in many ways, but motherhood *is* life-changing, and the changes didn't seem very profound to me. Sure, I stopped going out and I gave up caring about my appearance or wearing decent clothes, but I didn't feel particularly sublimated or invisible (of course there are moments when we all feel these things, for whatever reasons). I didn't feel like I was purposefully neglecting myself, but instead was simply consumed with caring for someone else – as well as running a house, sustaining a marriage, cooking daily meals, trying to do a bit of work, making a garden (gardening helped me cope with my grief and wasn't something I would give up) – the daily tasks and chores that nearly all women have to attend to. Anyway, our relationship didn't seem overly intense to me, it just seemed natural and sometimes tiring and mostly lovely. I felt like a normal, busy, scruffy mum, the sort of mum I'd more or less imagined I'd be.

So it wasn't me who decided to change the dynamic between us when Rose hit two. It was her, though if anything she turned the volume up. If I was the one she had always demanded and clung to, suddenly I was the one she was going to punish and rail against, then demand and cling to again. She certainly didn't give her dad an easy time of it, but it was me she focused on. The day would begin early – she woke at 5am – and with a tantrum, for whatever reason. The blinds in our bedroom would be down. Or up. If her dad went to get her morning milk, she would scream that she wanted me to get it. If I did it, she would shout that it should have been her dad. If I had a shower, there would be shouting. If she was carried the 'wrong' way, there would be shouting. If one of us went downstairs at the 'wrong' moment or if I wore the 'wrong' top, there would be shouting. There would be no appeasing her, and mostly we wouldn't concede to her demands, so the shouting would go on until she wore herself (and us) out. On Christmas morning she shouted so much about something – whatever it was – that she didn't open her stocking, about which there had been so much excitement, until the evening.

Most days, she shouted a lot in the day too. Again, for whatever reason. A toy wouldn't work, her clothes were wrong, she didn't want to hang up her coat. Mostly, it was about me doing something 'wrong'. I left the room or shut the loo door or didn't shut the loo door or used the wrong tone of voice. Of course, none of these things was what was really bothering her. What was really bothering her was a series of things which conspired to make her feel awful and, unable to contain her feelings at two years old, she let them explode out of her.

One of the big problems was that she was nearly always hungry (she was a good eater until she was eighteen months old, when, almost overnight, she simply started rejecting all food), which was probably why she woke so early (and her very low blood sugar first thing presumably prompted that first tantrum), which meant she was often overtired, which in turn led to her getting run down and feeling generally lousy. Sometimes she'd get ulcers all over her tongue, which made her feel even worse and so want to eat even less. Of course I tried to fix all these problems, but it's hard to get a child who won't eat to eat. A small pot of yoghurt would be a triumph. A tiny breadstick would make me happy. I knew that once she'd had a few bites of toast, things would get easier in the morning, but in practice it took ages to get any breakfast down her at all.

Plus, she was two. It's what two-year-olds do. They shout and rail and hit and storm. It's called the 'terrible twos' by everyone because it's such a typical rite of passage. Two-year-olds are frustrated for all kinds of reasons: they are learning to speak but can't yet communicate all their needs quickly and clearly enough; they realise how big the world is and they want to get at it, but they don't yet have the equipment or courage for the amount of independence they think they seek. And they are simply learning the rules and codes of behaviour, and there is no other way to learn these other than by testing them out over and over again.

I knew all this. I'd talked to other parents, I'd witnessed other children going through it, I'd read about it. Rose's terrible twos were bad, but they weren't *weirdly* bad. The not eating thing definitely made mornings worse than those of many of my peers, but she never hit or pushed other children, for example, which is what a good number of tots do. She was still, between the tantrums, delightful in all kinds of ways and I enjoyed those times immensely.

It's just that, more often than I wished, I couldn't handle the tantrums. I'd try, and often succeed. In the mornings or when my husband was around, I'd be firm and patient and rational: a parent, in other words. But just as often, I wouldn't cope well at all. If I was by myself and the tantrums began again after yet another unsuccessful lunch had passed, my patience would wear thin. That's when she and I would get into this horrible cycle: me worn down, her determined, both of us beside ourselves. I never hit her, but I had to stop myself. I would have to carry her upstairs for her time-outs over and over again, and then hold the door shut with all my might as she unleashed her angry energy on the door handle. I would try to gather myself and ignore her until she calmed down, but she hated to be ignored and so would hit me or scream in my face, until finally I would do something which jolted us both into silence.

I would lose my temper. I understand that expression now. I would literally lose control of myself for the first time, really, in my life. I'd hold my daughter by the shoulders and shout into her face to shut up. I'd call her a 'brat' and spit the word out. I told her she was a 'silly bitch'. I didn't decide to call her a silly bitch, the words just came out, and frankly, I wanted to call her something a lot worse. Sometimes I'd cry. In short, I became like a two-year-old.

When my daughter threw my words back in my face I realised with unbearable clarity that I was behaving in exactly the way I didn't believe a mother should: out of control, angry, impatient, abusive, childish. And far from it helping my daughter's rages, it was making things worse. She was imitating me, as children are programmed to do, and anyway, she was right. What did I expect?

Cataloguing the way we both behaved over many months in a few paragraphs makes it sound worse than it probably was, but still, it was bad. The terrible twos *are* bad. Some parents are better at handling it than others, just as some children are more difficult than others. Rose was on the tricky side for sure, and I definitely didn't rise to the occasion. But for every stalwart I've met, the good folk who manage never to raise their voices, there is someone else who will tell you that their son or daughter's tantrum phase nearly broke up their marriage, or had them, too, in frequent tears or pushed them over or close to some hitherto unknown edge. Finding these fellow parents and talking about our common flailing was a help, even if you had to break through a coded way of talking to get to the real truth. 'X is a nightmare? So is Rose. Did it drive you crazy? Did you crumble? Did you ever cry? You didn't? Never cried once? OK, next.'

The other thing to note is that many mothers are either pregnant with their second child when their first one hits the tricky stage, or caring for a new baby that has already arrived. I seemed always to be pregnant, highly hormonal and feeling terrible when Rose was a young toddler, first with a child who died in utero at sixteen weeks (I know), and then, a few months later, with Charlie Ray, who was born in October 2012 after yet another worrying pregnancy involving a weekly scan and daily hormone doses. He is, as I write this, two years old and an entirely different kind of child to Rose.

Everything got easier once Charlie was born. Of course, practically and physically, having two children is more work. You no longer have any time to yourself at all. But, much more significantly, I was no longer pregnant, no longer on weird drugs, no longer feeling chronically sick or chronically worried. I felt like myself again. Presumably, I became calmer. Rose also got easier. She hit her third birthday and things changed quickly. Every day she'd get easier. She'd let her dad put her to bed, she'd eat a relatively decent (for her) meal, she began to learn to use her scooter. She started a ballet class and trotted in without me. She also started a new nursery and loved it, and leaving her there each day was easy, which meant in one fell swoop we'd cut out one major, daily bout of crying, which in turn helped her break her habit of crying all the time. Quite quickly, we both began to feel more in control of our moods, and so the vicious circle – of her behaving badly, me reacting badly, her then behaving worse, both of us becoming beside ourselves – came to an end.

Of course, Rose still has the odd meltdown. She is still quick to cry, especially if she hurts herself or thinks she may have hurt herself (when she's tired she often claims to stub her toe, which is clearly her shorthand for saying, 'I need comforting, I don't know why, I just do'), and she still doesn't like it if I go out without her. But actually, just last week both her dad and I were able to leave her before bedtime in the care of her eighteen-year-old half-sister (whom she has always adored), without any tears at all. Two days ago she asked to have a shower and she enjoyed it: a big step, as for a long time showering was a habitual trigger point which inevitably led to her exploding with rage, tears pouring out of her as she descended into despair.

Oh, the descents into despair! Over a shower! Or, on my part, over a two-year-old playing up. What were we thinking? Well, we weren't thinking. We couldn't think. We were both ruled by our moods, by our hormones, by hunger, by worry, by fear, by tiredness, by feeling overwhelmed, by feeling out of control. But it doesn't seem to have done either of us any harm. Rose doesn't seem to have any real memories of our set-tos, and her manners and behaviour now are certainly as good as most of her peers. I remember it, yes, but can hardly believe it. I cried a lot? Really? I mean, Charlie is beginning to test his own boundaries now (and, of course, I realise he's only just begun), but the idea of dissolving in a heap about his disobedience or the fact that sometimes he hits me when he is frustrated baffles me. And yet I did it once, I know.

And, no doubt, I'll do it again. I remember my own adolescence well enough to know that stormy weather lies ahead, and I mention that milestone only because I know that, like a lunar eclipse, it's written in stone on the calendar of our lives. The rest, ahead, is blank, and no doubt will herald all kinds of ups and downs. My daughter and I haven't sworn at each other for about two years. I'd write 'long may it last', but those are famous last words.

1 A friend gave me a mantra to chant, given to her by her own mother who'd borne and brought up four children: 'Everything changes, nothing stays the same.' It's *so* true. So just ride, or try to ride, the wave. Things *will* change. Your child won't eat? That will change. Won't get in the bath? That will change. Has terrible tantrums? That will change. Sometimes it takes a long time – OK, so I didn't manage my first stress-free shower until my daughter was nearly four – and sometimes it happens quickly, but things do change.

2 The other really useful mantra, however clichéd, is: 'You do what's best for the unit.' If breastfeeding/terry-cloth nappies/a strict routine/whatever makes you unhappy, think again. Think about the unit's needs and happiness rather than just the baby's.

3 Also clichés, but also truer than it's possible to state are: 'Whatever gets you through the day', 'You

just muddle through' and, finally, 'It all comes out in the wash.'

4 Your experience is yours alone. You'll find fellow parents you can relate to and who will help you – you'll help each other – muddle through, and this is great. But it only goes so far. Sometimes I couldn't understand why I couldn't be as calm as a close pal, who seemed to be entirely unflappable. But the truth was that Rose was more difficult than her daughter. I didn't know this at the time and assumed I was a more crap parent than my friend, but I know now because I've had a difficult baby (Rose) and an easy one (Charlie). It's much easier to stay calm with Charlie than it was with Rose. Of course, on top of this, my friend may also have better parenting skills than me, but that's a separate thing.

5 Never buy anything for your child unless you need it right now. The cute sweater you buy in summer, because you can't resist it, won't fit come autumn, or will simply be rejected. The snowsuit you buy in advance, to be prepared, will go unused because it won't snow. And so on. I learned this the hard way. You can *always* buy a snowsuit at the last minute. From me, if necessary. Pristine, expensive, never used.

27 Things I Wish I'd Known Before I Had my First Child

By Emma Freud

Emma Freud, who has four children, is Director of Red Nose Day, and has been working with Comic Relief for over twenty years together with her partner, the film-maker Richard Curtis. Emma was a co-creator of the Make Poverty History campaign and a producer of the Live 8 concerts, and in 2011 she was awarded an OBE for her services to charity. She is also a TV and radio presenter for the BBC, writes for the *Guardian*, *The Sunday Times* and *Tatler* and for the last twenty years has worked with Richard as script editor or co-producer on *Four Weddings and a Funeral*, *Bridget Jones' Diary*, *Notting Hill*, *Love Actually*, *The Vicar of Dibley* and *About Time*. She'd quite like a little lie down now.

There is no life experience which prompts total strangers to tell you how to behave quite like having babies. I have seen perfectly polite, kind, intelligent people cross the room to give lengthy unasked-for advice on impending motherhood to pregnant women they have never met. I've known mothers who impart guidance with so much judgement that I have felt my life was being marked out of ten by a panel with scorecards. I've experienced gentle grannies giving me 'tips' on how to stop my baby crying, which have felt so critical that they've reduced me to sobs louder than my child's.

And the irony is that in trying to tell you all the things I wish I had known four children ago, I realise I am turning myself into one of those ghastly people. However, I am justifying this chapter with the knowledge that the most comforting part of having a crap day as a mum, where you feel you are single-handedly prepping your child for the psychiatrist's couch, is when you ring a friend and they tell you that they are also still in their pyjamas at 3pm, having fed their two-year-old Haribo for breakfast AND lunch.

So if you have a moment and need a bit of support, do read this, but dismiss anything which doesn't chime, and imagine I am saying it in the most loving, unassuming, gentle voice you know … a bit like Olivia Colman, Pam Ayres or Ruth in *The Archers*. This is not about criticism – and whatever you're already doing is probably brilliant – but here are some of the many lessons I learned way too late. It would make me supremely happy to think that my arsing up will mean you don't have to.

Pregnancy

Emotional hypersensitivity is part of the lovely gift nature gives pregnant women, only second in fun to the onset of piles. It comes with a tendency to make things mean something entirely different to what was intended. For example:

FRIEND SAYS: You're eight months pregnant? Wow, you're tiny!
YOU THINK: My baby is underdeveloped and has probably just died.

Or

FRIEND SAYS: You're eight months pregnant? Wow, you look so healthy!
YOU THINK: She thinks I'm obese, and that my unborn child must be so overweight that it will no longer fit through the birth canal and will have to be airlifted out using a winch.

During your pregnancy, whenever you can't feel the baby move you may find yourself worrying that *something has gone horribly wrong*. Don't, as I did, buy a stethoscope to check its heartbeat – they're really difficult to work unless you're medically trained. And when you can't hear the baby's heartbeat with the stethoscope you did buy, don't, as I did, buy another more expensive one in case that works better. It doesn't and you will find, as I did, that they are really hard to sell back on eBay. In fact, if you really want one, I still have two.

Do *find out as much as possible about childbirth* while

you're pregnant via books, the internet or classes. It may not end up being relevant to your own labour, but it will give you ammunition so that when 'friends' tell you a birth horror story ('they used a sink plunger to pull him out') you will have a medical context to put it in ('it's called a ventouse and is less painful than forceps').

Don't forget to read a couple of chapters on *what to do with the baby once it's born*. It's very easy to use all your energy learning about the birth (which lasts about one day) and forget to learn about looking after the thing that gets born (which lasts about 81 years).

Childbirth

When you go into labour, you may find that you become meek, apologetic and not as feisty as usual. Alternatively, you may turn into Motherzilla. My current boyfriend got lost driving the car on the way to the hospital for the birth of our son and has still not forgiven me for shouting at him: 'YOU ONLY HAD TO DO *ONE* THING!'

You may *vomit during the labour*. I was terrified of this happening, but when it did, it's wasn't nearly as bad as I thought it would be. Your body just goes into efficient 'eject mode' and you find yourself going with it. Don't stress about this.

On the other hand, while trying as hard as you can to push out something the size of a pineapple, *you may poo*. There's nothing good I can say about this, just know that it might happen. And don't tell anyone if it does – you will get over it, but they won't.

If you have a *caesarean*, there will be between eight and twenty people in the operating theatre with you. It doesn't mean that anything has gone wrong, and none of them is the priest waiting to give you last rites, but it's a surprising number of people to be looking at your insides if you aren't expecting them.

First days

Whatever your child looks like, you may find yourself crying at some point in the hospital because *everyone else's babies are so ugly*, whereas yours is so lovely. Just know that everyone thinks that about their babies too, and feels sorry for you for having such a minger.

Your front bottom will be sore, obviously, and weeing will sting for a few days. *When you need a wee*, run a couple of inches of warm water in a bath. Sit in the bath and wee there and it won't sting at all, then use a hairdryer on 'cold' to dry off – it's much gentler than a towel. Sounds weird, but you will LOVE me for this when it happens.

Know that on *day three you will cry* because you think something has gone terribly wrong, whereas you are actually crying because your milk has come in. Also know that some women only cry on day three, but others (like me) cry every day for two months. It gets easier.

Stay in pyjamas for the first week, or two if you possibly can. It reminds other people that you've just been through a massive experience, and that they should make you a cup of tea. And it reminds you to be kind to yourself. If people say, 'Is there anything I can do?' say YES and give them a list that includes filling your fridge and doing the hoovering. People are so in awe/terrified of new mothers that they will tend to do your bidding. As soon as the clothes go on, Mr Sheen will be all yours again.

Write down what *your baby's character* is like at the end of the first week. You'll think it's obvious and that all babies are pretty much the same, but they aren't. I did this with all four of my children – and each time their baby characteristics were astonishingly close to the great big humans I now live with.

Amazingly, *their poo really is meant to be that colour*. The first one is pitch black. Then all poos are fluorescent yellow until you start feeding your baby solids, at which point they go brown (the poo, not the baby). N.B. If it's green, this is nature's way of telling you they have a tummy ache, though you would probably know this already thanks to the lovely screaming noise you can hear in your ears.

No matter how big or securely fastened the nappy, you will still frequently get a *poo-right-up-the-back-of-the-vest* situation. It helps to get vests with envelope necks so you can pull the pooed-up vest down to take it off, rather than a vest with a round neck which means you end up with neon-coloured faeces all over the back of the baby's head as well.

Babies tend to cry for five main reasons: hunger, tiredness, teething, wind or they've pooed themselves. It's IMPOSSIBLE to know the difference between the crying noises unless you are Gina Ford. But if you feel your baby has been well enough fed and burped, it's most likely to be tiredness that makes them cry. Try putting them to sleep instead of giving them more milk – it took me years to work that one out.

Know that *EVERYONE is just muddling through.* No one really knows how to do it. They all make you think they do. But they don't. Everyone struggles for the first three months, and all the beaming parents in magazines are bastards. If your baby is still alive, you are probably doing no worse than anyone else. I actually tore my copy of Gina Ford in half one day and threw it across the room because it was making me feel so inadequate and my baby wouldn't do the things the book said it was meant to. The whole newborn phase tends to be about finding the balance between you telling your baby what you want it to do, and it telling you what it's going to do. One of you will win in the end, but it takes a while to work out that pole position. If you're able to get your baby into a routine (i.e. you win), it's incredibly helpful. But if you just can't, don't beat yourself up. The first few weeks are always chaotic but you just keep trying and learning and listening to the baby, and at some point things click into some sort of place. Though when your partner has slept on the sofa for a year so as not to disturb Young Mussolini, you can probably assume you didn't get the balance quite right after all.

First year

When you are six months old, *the washing machine* is as interesting as the TV. Put your baby in front of a cold rinse cycle if you need a break.

Encourage your baby to form its big attachment to a *muslin square* rather than a cashmere blanket or a bunny. Way easier to replace when it gets left under the sofa/on a train/in a public loo/on a street corner/in another country. FedEx's loss will be your gain.

When you start *feeding your baby solids*, the mess is literally staggering. A bib can't contain the extensive and expert distribution of mushed-up food that a baby is able to provide, and it doesn't make for a relaxed mealtime if you are worrying about the bright orange stains on a favourite baby outfit. Try ditching all clothes and giving the meal while your baby is just wearing a nappy, then do the bath straight afterwards. Or for total ease, actually feed them in the bath.

Don't spend too long *making baby food* – it's a relative waste of time and you will mind too much if it doesn't work out. Pureeing fruit and veg occasionally is enough. I remember once taking an hour and a half to make baby fish pie for my daughter. She took one mouthful and spat it out, and I looked into having her adopted. The awfulness of that day was my own fault for investing too much love and time into some haddock.

Later on ...

There's a real contradiction with the early days of parenting. Your maternal instincts kick in so hard that you find yourself *abandoning your own needs* and giving everything you've got to the baby. Refer to: a pristine baby with immaculate bedding in a sparkling buggy on its way to a playgroup being pushed by a bedraggled mother wearing slippers and leaking milk into an ancient onesie. It's surprisingly easy to let this happen, but it can be a recipe for problems later, as the self-sacrifice can end up becoming self-neglect, frustration and latent anger. It's worth remembering that bit in a plane safety talk where the steward says: 'In the event of an emergency, put an oxygen mask on yourself before putting one on your child.' They're right. Unless you're looking after your own needs (emotional, professional, playful and hygienic), you won't be creating a cogently balanced environment or modelling self-respect to your kids, and your child will have a tougher time learning how to thrive. Much as it goes against a new mother's grain, you have to put yourself first whenever you can. Oh, I've gone all Freudian on you. Sorry.

1 Get a *Hippychick* seat. They are like reinforced bumbags worn round your waist and your baby uses it as a hip-seat from 3–18 months. I can't lie to you, it looks a bit weird, but it will totally protect your back and save you hundreds of pounds in osteopath bills later on. Promise.

2 *Top drug advice*: if your baby is poorly and paracetamol isn't cutting it, you are allowed to use both Calpol and ibuprofen if you need to, as long as you don't give them at the same time. Give the normal amount of Calpol, and two hours later give the normal amount of ibuprofen, then two hours later give the normal amount of Calpol again and so on until the worst is over. You can check the NHS website for more details.

3 The better the TV programme, the more likely the child in your arms is to *puke*.

4 However much people may seem interested in your baby, they aren't really, they're just being nice. Try not to bore your friends with *baby progress* – put it on Instagram or Twitter or Facebook so you feel you've shared it, and then keep quiet.

5 And finally, *trust your instincts*. Actually, deep down, when everything else gets stripped away, you know how to do it and you know what is logical and right for your child. In my view, make sure all roads point to the quality of kindness. Not much else really matters. Good luck, and look after yourself.

Single Plus One

By Anne Marie Scanlon

Anne Marie Scanlon is a journalist and author of *It's Not Me … It's You*. She lives in Henley with her seven-year-old son, Jack.

I always feel like a bit of a fraud when I tick the 'single' box on official forms enquiring about my marital status. I am not married and never have been, but although I'm not in a relationship I don't feel single. In my mind I stopped being 'single' when I had my son seven years ago. Officially I'm a 'single mother' or 'lone parent' (the politically correct term *du jour*). However, as any woman with a small child will tell you, I am neither alone, nor single – I am a 'plus one'.

For many people, the term 'single mother' conjures up a *Pramface/Daily Mail* stereotype of a younger, uneducated girl, encased in velour and living on a sink estate. But when I became pregnant I was in my late thirties, living in New York with a Master's degree and a career, and I didn't own a stitch of leisure wear or velour clothing.

My life was fine. I had no plans to change it. I was single, and happy not to permanently integrate another person into my immediate future. I certainly wasn't planning on becoming pregnant (I'd had problems in previous years and thought the fertility boat had sailed). But on Mother's Day 2006 I was deeply shocked to find out that I was 'in the family way'. In that moment my life changed. Irrevocably. It didn't matter what happened afterwards – whether I became a mother or didn't become a mother, that blue line had changed everything. I was in a relationship, but it was unsteady and unstable and had no future (which had been fine by me). We were off and on more times than the light in an overeater's fridge.

I thought, like everyone else in the same situation, that I'd have time to prepare for the changes in my life. It didn't work out that way. Even before I'd taken the test I'd been feeling perpetually nauseous. The doctors assured me it would pass, so I waited. It didn't pass. Every day it got slightly worse. Then the vomiting began. By the time I was three months pregnant I was wretchedly ill. I had lost over a stone in weight (eight pounds alone in one week, which under normal circumstances would have thrilled me), I could not eat, I threw up countless times during the day and had started waking up in the middle of the night for the express purpose of being sick. My on–off boyfriend didn't see (or perhaps didn't wish to see) that this was not a normal pregnancy, and he wasn't around much to help.

During this period I was admitted to hospital three times. They topped me up with fluids and sent me home with oral anti-sickness medication which I would swallow and then promptly vomit back up. I did nothing, and indeed could do nothing, but lie in bed waiting for the sickness to pass, as the doctors kept assuring me it would. At the twelve-week mark I was malnourished and dehydrated; both my body and brain were long past working properly. I could not function and, despite the best efforts of friends, I needed full-time care. I needed my mother. I was wheeled onto the plane at JFK and wheeled off at Heathrow where Mum met me and took me to her home in Henley-on-Thames.

The following morning I woke up in a pool of blood. We had a half-hour drive to the hospital in Reading, and I was so ill that I could barely sit upright in the seat. I was terrified that I was miscarrying, yet at the same time I remember wondering just how long it would be after the miscarriage that I would stop feeling sick.

At the hospital the doctors informed me that I was on the verge of a coronary and admitted me straight away. The doctor thought I didn't understand his diagnosis. 'You could drop dead at any second,' he said, 'it's that serious.' I knew it was serious. I just didn't care anymore. I'd had enough. I couldn't take feeling that bad for much longer.

My life had just changed again and I didn't know it. I was in hospital for a week then discharged with a large bag of medication which I had to take for the remainder of my pregnancy. My condition needed constant monitoring, so there was no question of me returning to New York. When the fog in my brain started to clear and the nausea and vomiting were controlled enough to let me think about something else I was very conflicted. I hadn't known when

I'd got on the plane at Kennedy with a weekend bag that I was actually leaving New York after twelve years. It was too sudden. I didn't have a chance to adjust. But at the same time, I was happy to be with my mother and feel safe and taken care of.

While the first trimester of my pregnancy had been an utter nightmare, the second trimester was like a dream. I had my Mammy taking care of me, I had old friends close by, it was the middle of summer and picturesque Henley was certainly more pleasant than steamy New York. But by my third trimester the realities started hitting home. I felt like the biggest failure on the planet. A failure as a person, as a professional, as a woman, as a daughter and, already, as a mother. My situation was hardly ideal. I was no longer a 'single gal' gadding about New York in high heels, writing about cosmetics and sex (my friends called me Carrie O'Bradshaw). Instead I was pregnant, single, pushing forty and living in my mother's spare room. How in the name of God had it come to this?

When I looked to baby books and antenatal classes for a crumb of comfort and consolation I felt even worse. Every single baby book I read reduced me to tears of rage, frustration and shame. One book said a blackout curtain for the 'nursery' was a non-negotiable essential. My child wasn't going to have a blackout curtain because he wasn't even going to have a nursery. All he was getting was a crib beside my bed in my mother's spare room. Oh yes, that negative voice in my head that often tells me I'm shit was having a ball. Similarly, every book I read assumed I had a 'partner' (very politically correct), and there were whole chapters devoted to this mythical partner. One book even informed me that I could milk my pregnancy and gouge 'my husband' for a nice big diamond ring. Oh how I laughed. Bitterly.

The antenatal classes were full of joyous happy couples – men and women delighted with themselves and their fertility. And me. And my mother. I made her come with me because I didn't want to be alone amid all the couples. My mother was quite surprised by this sudden neediness – I'm an only child and am used to going it alone, and walking into a room by myself has rarely fazed me. But that was before I was pregnant and alone.

The class was overheated and long and boring, and the men did most of the talking. It was about this time that I started wearing my late grandmother's engagement and wedding ring on a chain around my neck. My mother was downright shocked by this sudden show of conformity. I was a bit shocked myself, but I felt very, pardon the dreadful pun, singled out. In New York single mothers in their thirties and forties are not that rare. As anyone who has ever seen *Sex and the City* will tell you, it's tough being a single lady in New York, so many women – aware that the biological clock is ticking – have IVF by donor, or adopt, or even get knocked up the old-fashioned way. In Henley I felt like the only single mother in the village. I don't think this is about nationality – I figure if I'd been in a small town in upstate New York I would have experienced the same sort of feelings – but that didn't make it any easier.

On the flip side, there were advantages to being an older expectant mother – the main one being that most of my friends had already given birth. One of them had two children, the first a 'natural' home birth and the second in hospital with the aid of an epidural. Having tried both extremes my friend told me in no uncertain terms that I was to demand pain relief and plenty of it.

She didn't have to try hard to convert me. Unusually for an Irish Catholic who spent thirteen years being educated by nuns, I don't believe pain makes you a better person, closer to God or more likely to dwell in paradise in the hereafter. The piety of martyrdom and suffering is simply propaganda – for centuries this ethos was used by the rich minority to keep the poor majority in their place. Amazingly in the 21st century it's now equally successful at keeping women in theirs. Once women gave birth and were lucky to survive the experience. Now we are judged on *how well* we give birth.

In the end, the labour was even more horrific than my worst imaginings (which were pretty bad it has to be said). At one point the epidural slipped out and the pain was so fierce that I had visual and auditory hallucinations. But, you know, if I'd been a 'good' girl and a 'proper' mother I would have just breathed through the pain and given birth the 'natural' way. 'Natural' these days has become synonymous with 'green' – everything natural is 'good' and 'wholesome' and ecologically sound. There's a certain breed of midwife who would have you believe that: a) there is no alternative to a lovely 'natural' birth at all;

and b) said 'natural' birth will be so serene you could do it in a lovely sunlit field surrounded by hopping bunnies and buttercups. People forget that nature is not just pretty birdsong and flowers, it is brutal and violent. It's not Disney, its Darwin.

I have met many women who think they did not give birth 'properly' because they had an emergency C-section, but when the doctors informed me they were going to perform one, I didn't beg them to rethink the idea. I did not care how my son arrived in this world, just that he got here safe, and I was damned if I was going to let any government body or website tell me I was less of a woman for doing so. Likewise, I was never bothered that some people thought I was a 'bad' mother for not exclusively breastfeeding. As far as I was concerned, my job as a mother, as a parent, was to see that my child was safe, warm, fed and cuddled. I ticked all those boxes and he thrived. The 'good' mothers and the government could all feck off.

Gosh, that makes me sound very strong and even quite militant. Yet it's funny that I should have been so immune to the opinions of others when it came to the birth and care of my child, because during my pregnancy I felt very exposed.

And wrong.

And guilty.

And dreadfully ashamed.

After the C-section my son and I stayed in hospital for five days. During that time I was acutely aware that all the other tiny babies in the ward had doting daddies and mine didn't. A photographer from the local paper came in and took pictures of all the new arrivals. 'And what's your husband's name?' he asked me. 'I'm not married.' 'Sorry,' he apologised, shaking his head at his own mistake, 'what's your partner's name?' The words 'I don't have a partner' nearly choked me. Oh God, having to say it out loud to a total stranger was terrible. At that moment I think I'd rather have admitted to being a mass murderer or a woman who shoves cats in bins.

Today, as a sane person who has not recently given birth and whose hormones are (relatively) stable, I know the photographer didn't give a damn one way or the other, but at the time, in the bed, I felt like Hester Prynn in *The Scarlet Letter*, with my shame pinned to my lapel for all the world to see. Yet, in true maternal fashion, it was *my* shame, not my son's. He was not the source of shame, just as my pregnancy (and not my baby) had made me ill. I felt exposed and vulnerable and a total failure as a woman because I did not have a man. Yet I was overwhelmed by love for my small baby and the absolute joy of his arrival.

And funnily enough, when I took my five-day-old son home, instead of mourning the lack of a man in my life I was actually relieved. I was so 'in love' with my baby I couldn't imagine having to accommodate another person into the arrangement. My mother certainly didn't expect emotional reassurance from me – she behaved like a mother and took care of me. Yet despite my mother doing all the housework, cooking, shopping and laundry, leaving me free to look after my baby, I was still permanently exhausted and dazed. Nothing can prepare you for looking after a tiny infant. Nothing. I laugh when I hear couples who are expecting their first child say that it will not impact their fabulous lives. They will continue to be utterly fabulous – they will take their children to fancy restaurants/trekking up the Andes/to Glastonbury. Oh no, the baby will not change things, it will be business as usual. Even before I had a child I knew this was nonsense. Pregnancy and childbirth inevitably bring change. Isn't that the point? Why do it otherwise?

Despite having my mother full-time, the first six weeks were difficult. I wish I had known then that it was only going to be six weeks, that it would pass. There was something else I wish I had known. Soon after returning from the hospital I looked at my tiny son lying in his crib and suddenly had an extremely vivid vision of putting a cushion over his face. A few days later the same thing happened again, only this time I imagined sticking a knife in his chest. These 'visions' absolutely terrified me. I loved my child and I certainly didn't want to harm him, but I was acutely aware of how vulnerable he was, how easily he could be hurt, damaged or killed. Was I going mad? I never said a word to anyone, terrified that my baby would be taken away and I'd end up in some sort of institution. The 'visions' passed as quickly as they came, but I never forgot them. Then when my son was eighteen months old I discovered that these episodes are relatively common for new mothers – they are not about a wish to harm the child but rather a way of foreseeing all the dangers. But of course, we're all under such pressure to have 'good' births and to be 'good' mothers that we daren't speak of this sort of thing or admit to having any sort of difficulties transitioning into our new roles.

For a while I bought into modern motherhood and strove towards maternal perfection, towards being a 'Professional Mother' (my definition of a woman who dedicates the same energy to childrearing as she once did to her career). I stocked up on recipe books, made healthy food and engaged in educational play. Finally, a combination of exhaustion and boredom drove me out of the competition.

I work from home, which is easier now my son has started school, but still means that I am also a full-time mother, which everybody knows is a full-time job in itself. By the time I've met my professional obligations, cooked, cleaned, done the laundry, tidied the garden and put out the bins, I am exhausted. Every night I read to my son. That's our 'special time', and even though I don't bake cakes for the never-ending fundraisers at school, produce fancy handicrafts or manage to put my make-up on every morning, my child is healthy and happy. Like all small children, he thinks the world revolves around him, yet he knows, thanks to me and the fact that I have interests beyond him, that there is bigger world out there. He's always been a curious child, and it delights me that he is so eager for information and experience.

But even though I have opted out of the Professional Mother Olympics, I am still not immune to the self-doubt and guilt that plague all parents. Am I doing it right? Is my son OK? Am I failing him? Am I letting him down? Will he spend a fortune on therapy because of my bad parenting? Add to that the guilt about bringing him into the world knowing he would not have a full-time father. *Aïe aïe aïe.* But then, sometimes, in the midst of imagining my worst fears, I come across a newspaper story about a child who has been used as a human ashtray, and I think I'm not actually all that bad.

In many ways I like being single (plus one). I've never been a great one for compromise and, while I don't have problems making decisions, I do not fare well with the decision-making *process.* While I do worry about my child missing out on having a full-time dad, it's only occasionally that I worry about my own unattached status. Going to the park on a Sunday usually triggers a bit of self-pity as my son and I are surrounded by dads. It would be nice for him to have a man to play with, and it would be nice for me to be able to have a little bit of time to myself. Then again, I don't think either my boy or I would take kindly to having another male around on a full-time basis. Although I'm fairly strict, my son and I have a lot of fun together, we tell each other silly stories, giggle and 'act the eejit' a lot. I didn't miss my child before I had him, but then again, I didn't know what I was missing.

THINGS I wish I'd Known

1 The best piece of advice I got while pregnant, and the one I always make sure to pass along to expectant mothers, came from a friend of mine with two children of her own. She told me to ignore people who say you can interpret your baby's cries. 'You can't tell if it's a "hungry cry" or a "tired cry",' she said. 'Anyone who says so is talking bollocks. Babies cry, it's what they do.' It's true.

2 During the first six weeks of my son's life I was pretty much a zombie. I don't do well without sleep at the best of times, but being woken several times a night quickly turned me into a shambling, drooling wreck. What made it worse was I'd heard endless horror stories from other women about how they didn't have an unbroken night's sleep, read a book or finish a meal for two years. Two years! I thought I would drop dead from exhaustion long before I reached the magical milestone of 24 months. Maybe I happen to know a lot of unlucky women (or indeed ladies slightly prone to exaggeration), but the unrelenting pace and exhaustion tapered off a bit after six weeks and a bit more with each passing month. I really wish I'd known that the zombie phase was going to be a relatively short one – it made it so much worse thinking there was no end in sight.

3 I wish I had known that other women lie. We live in a culture of competitive maternity and women are held up to ridiculous standards from the moment they conceive. Once the baby is born the competition becomes increasingly fierce – the rate at which your child thrives and hits their milestones is viewed as a direct reflection on your ability as a mother. So when someone tells you that their baby is sleeping through the night at two months old, remember that their definition of sleeping through the night may not tally with yours.

4 My advice to any expectant mother would be to ignore what the other mummies are saying and doing. A baby is not a baby for very long. Why spoil the experience by holding yourself up to impossible standards, and why make yourself miserable by comparing yourself to the front that someone else is putting up? Your job as a mother is to keep your baby safe, fed, clean and loved. That's all. They'll clap and wave in their own time.

Bite Me, Baby Experts

By Afsaneh Knight

Afsaneh Knight is a novelist. She lives in London with her husband, Rupert, and their two children, Atticus, aged eight, and Irsia, aged six.

Before having children I didn't, as a general rule, go in for shame. So I made myself look like a huge baboon's arse – so what? We're a race of nerds, us humans, walking into lamp posts and fishing out wedgies and speaking in stupid accents when we think nobody's listening. We all fall over. Get up, and don't dwell on it.

I only have one lone pre-child memory, in my entire vault of ignominy, which makes me want to run screaming down the street with shame. It occurred in Soho Square at 3am, which is a mitigating factor; everybody existing in Soho Square at 3am either has done or is about to do something absolutely humiliating. My chosen act of grinding mortification was to try – *try*, note thee – to do a high kick over the handlebars of a parked motorcycle. I said 'wooh!' as I attempted it. Yes, I did.

Post-breeding, however, my life for a time turned into one gigantic, linear shame-fest – memories so butt-clenchingly heinous that, even now, I can't let them go. While admittedly, during the baby epoch, I had the real and mighty excuse of hormones in my corner, the fact remains – hormones or no – that I sat in a chair and went through Gina Ford with a highlighter.

I went through that lunatic, barren manual – on how to keep a baby alive with dark curtains and alarm clocks, but without the quietest whisper of love – with a pink highlighter pen. I did that. Me. My son was curled inside me, a perfect, dorky little dragon about to take flight, and there I sat, highlighting Gina Ford as if I were revising for an A-Level. And where the hell, thinking about it, did I even get a highlighter from? Who has highlighters? Ah, Christ. The shame – my shame – is like glue; no escaping.

When Atticus was born (hauled out yelling, poor thing, by ventouse), Gina Ford was in my hospital bag, as if my exquisite boy, startled and skinny and beautiful as a hare, were a piece of equipment. There were my highlighted passages, full of millilitres, grams, hours and minutes – instructions as dead and ridiculous as instructions for falling in love, as instructions for grieving, as instructions for feeling joy.

It took me nearly a month, more's my shame, to deliver that book to its spiritual home in the trash. I knew what my baby needed: he needed me. He needed the sound of my voice and the beat of my heart, he needed to be near me, tucked into some part of me, for as long as the world was strange to him. But the book said I had to put him down, alone, for a 30-minute sleep at ten o'clock precisely, and, shame of shames, I listened. For three weeks I muzzled my roaring instinct, and deferred.

Atticus howled in confusion, baffled by the capricious timetable into which he was being shoehorned. And I despaired. My baby didn't want to sleep when he was *supposed* to sleep, he was hungry when he wasn't *supposed* to be hungry, and I surely was the greatest, shiniest, most bubonic failure of a mother in the entire history of reproduction, unable to follow the simplest recipe on how to bake a happy baby. (A 'contented' baby, says Ms Ford – not even happy. Contented! Screw that! When my babies laughed they laughed from the deep as if their diaphragms would burst.)

One long, unhappy night I stood leaning against the bedroom wall, back aching, alternately singing and bouncing and whispering 'please, please sleep' to Atticus, who was uncomfortably awake in my arms. He was fretful (obviously, with such a tool of a mother) and scrabbling at his newly acquired eczema. Everything around was silent, everything dark, and Atticus and I were the only two people awake in the world. Except, maybe, for somebody sad standing on a bridge.

Some bit of me bigger than my brain swelled up, a life raft and a whistle – *enough*, it blew. *Enough of this.*

Enough, I thought. *Enough.*

I built a fortress of pillows around my sleeping husband, I lay down with Atticus in the crook of my arm, and I cried onto his tufty head while I fed him. He smelled, as always, of toast and honey and candles and biscuits and gardens and sweet milk. As he fell asleep I watched his eyes flutter shut like beating wings – and then I slept, too, and when I woke it was morning, and there he was, pale and still and peaceful. Would you believe me if I told you that my son has the most beautiful eyes in the world? They are round and huge and at times almost black and at times the colour of the sun. When he opened his eyes that morning, I was what he saw, and his world that day was brave and safe.

The book went in the bin. I had learned my lesson.

Or not at all, as the case actually was.

More shame, more shame to come.

A month later, Atticus's little tummy was filling with air after every feed. It would inflate, and Atticus would cry – scream, in fact – and contort, and arch his back in pain.

'Wind,' said the health visitor.

'It's constant,' I said.

'You need to burp him,' said the health visitor.

'I do,' I said.

'It's wind,' said the health visitor.

'He's in pain,' I said.

'Wind,' said the health visitor.

I knew it wasn't wind. My tiny son would spend a large part of each day and night weeping, and eventually I would weep with him – unable to help the person I loved most in the world, loved so much my heart pummelled at my ribs like a boxer.

But the health visitor insisted: *wind*. And my voice inexplicably left me; I didn't speak up.

In my confusion, I tried to do what I could. I took Atticus to see a cranial osteopath recommended by a London maternity hospital. The cranial osteopath told me that I needed to 'de-stress' Atticus's stomach, and I should feed him only once every four hours.

'But it's 35 degrees,' I said, referring to the record-breaking heatwave that was then clouting the life out of the country – people were sticking to things and dying and melting into pools of tar on the pavements.

'Once every three and a half hours, then,' smiled the cranial osteopath, 'maximum.'

That afternoon, Atticus and I paced in the steaming jungle of our kitchen. He was red and hot and livid with thirst, and I, for an hour that was in fact a decade in Soul Years, denied him milk. *It will make him sick if I feed him*, I told myself, *it will hurt him, it will stress his stomach*. I stood, rocking him desperately, sweat running into my eyes, staring at the clock – *only one hour and 57 minutes left, only one hour and 57 minutes ...*

Toward the end of that toxic hour, my last worm of sanity dug through, and I threw the clock on the sofa – would have gone at it with a sledgehammer, had one been handy – and I sat down, and I fed my baby. He was thirsty again an hour later, and so I fed him again. And through the mulch of tiredness and anxiety and sadness, I knew that sitting by the open window with Atticus drowsy on my chest was where I was supposed to be. I was doing what I was meant to be doing.

Nobody else knew a thing about my baby. The apparent

experts with their voodoo advice – they knew nothing of Atticus, of his long fingers and his downy ears, of the way he flinched at loud noises and held my gaze for minutes; they knew nothing of how it felt to be loved by him. Every day since Atticus was born I've woken up exactly two minutes before he does. Even now, eight years on. My eyes flick open, I reach for my phone and check the time, and two minutes later the quiet in the house breaks – snuffle snuffle, creak, pad pad pad pad pad, thump thump thump thump thump – and he appears by my bed, lion cub smile, utterly delighted to see me, still, after all this time. He came from the guts of me, my little boy, and even his silences I hear like songs; how could anyone know how to care for him but me?

I knew it wasn't wind, I knew his stomach didn't need 'de-stressing' – Atticus, it turned out, had severe allergies, hence the writhing, the screaming, the inflated stomach, the eczema. That discovery was a sunrise in his life, and in mine.

'You are going to be fine,' I told him, 'and better than fine. You are a small dragon, and you are going to fly.'

Within weeks I had a baby who was putting on weight and dozing snugly in his cot, fat fists relaxed above his head. A baby who – fancy that – was having regular naps and regular feeds and (almost!) sleeping through the night. Quite naturally he and I found our way there, without bookfuls of trademarked methods and branded timetables.

I knew how to protect him and how to nurture him, and, more than this, I knew how to make him smile – that wide smile that was, and is, like an egg cracking, like the day dawning. My lucky daughter – by the time she arrived, 23 months after Atticus, I was equipped, backboned, ready to pace my circle around her and snarl at all comers. I had found my voice by then, which is to say – my roar. Becoming a mother makes lionesses of us.

But poor Atticus had to tolerate a few more instances of mouse mothering, before I stood up and growled – I was still squeaking into my hands like a geisha, like a giggler, like a cheese. I remember a friend visiting – she came breezing off the Hammersmith and City line and clamped her unwashed hands around Atticus's face, stroking, caressing, massaging tube effluvium into every one of his immaculate newborn pores.

Did I say, loudly, 'Any tube seat ever tested has been found to carry traces of every type of human secretion – semen, shit, sweat, spit and piss. You're currently kneading that into my baby's face. *Stop it*, for God's sake'?

No. I did not. Instead I stood mutely horrified, and accepted a jaunty double kiss from said filthy friend without having uttered a word.

I also allowed my mother to take Atticus to see some 100 per cent charlatan, batshit, burping Korean monks – 'monks' – who she discovered boiling their snake oil off Regent's Street. My mother is one of life's believers and enthusers, and she successfully trounced every one of our childhood illnesses with a combination of arnica tablets, chamomile tea and her own iron, enchanter's will. She reckoned a bit of healing for Atticus, who had had a tough entry to planet earth, could do no harm, and thus my husband

and I found ourselves holding our thoroughly perplexed one-year-old on our laps while Master Mim (or somesuch), an unsmiling ferret in a t'ai chi onesie, placed his hands on Atticus and did massive, startling belches into the air, explaining mid-BAAAAAAARP that the 'toxins' in Atticus were being transferred to him, and then duly expressed through the medium of GIANT FUCKING BURPS.

My mother had pre-paid six sessions for Atticus, but I told her we would not be returning, with my husband clarifying: 'If that burping psycho ever comes near my son again, I'll punch him in the face.'

We strapped Atticus – the most toxin-free, pure, trusting and delightful person you'll ever meet – into his bright red pushchair, let him examine the shoe cubbies near the entrance (which appealed to him exceedingly) allowed him to press the buttons in the lift (which was always a treat) had appalled, snorting laughter fits as the lift went down, and then went to a café for fluffy milk and rice cakes.

The gassy monks were the last of it – the last of my timidity and the end of my Era of Shame. I bucked up. I realised that as my son relied on me to speak for him, my voice had better be strong.

Of course, there remain the small shames that every mother carries through the day – of having snapped unfairly, of running inexcusably late, of having forgotten a promise to superglue a toy or buy crisps. But, oh, these are nothing. These are stumbles made in the chaos of love, they are part of being a lioness. You have your tail pulled and your heart fledged, your whiskers kissed and your head used as a pillow. Sometimes you bat away with too firm a paw – but no harm done. Blow the blunders to the wind.

An old, dear friend of mine recently had a lovely little boy.

'You're going to have to teach me how to look after a baby,' she said when pregnant.

'I've got no idea,' I said. 'I have no idea who you're going to get. I could tell you how to look after *my* babies, but that wouldn't be much help.'

Only she knows how to look after her son. Not me, not anybody else. She may fuss and doubt and follow bad advice, but she will soon realise that her love, the fierceness of it, is all she needs. There may be long nights, long weeks, but the truth is having children is like waking up. How much more beautiful life is, here in the daylight.

1 That other people may be experts on looking after their own child, but not yours. Only you know how to do that.

2 That the tiredness will end. When you're dragging yourself around by your fingernails, it's easy to think

that you will NEVER SLEEP FOR MORE THAN 45 MINUTES AGAIN. You will.

3 That flying from London to Australia with a one-year-old and a three-year-old is a bad, bad, bad, bad idea.

4 That it is best to choose godparents who are single and childless.

5 That if you're unhappy, your baby will be unhappy. If you're happy, your baby will be happy. It's that simple.

The Breastfeeding Queen Who Never Was

By Bryony Gordon

Bryony Gordon is a feature writer for the *Telegraph*. She lives in London with her husband, Harry, and their one-year-old daughter, Edie.

Day three without any sleep, and I am lying almost naked in a hospital bed unable to move my legs. Complete strangers prod me here, there and everywhere. In particular, though, they are prodding my breasts. They have squeezed and squished them, crushed and pinched them, and now the redness of my nipples is only matched by the redness of my eyes, finally dry after hours of tears. But I can't cry any more, I think. There is almost nothing left in me. I have given literally everything I have.

Over the last 72 hours I have been drugged and numbed with an injection into my spine. Twice. I have watched my own blood pour over the hospital floor as the drip into my hand came undone. I have vomited and hovered over a cardboard bedpan, trying not to squash it or wee all over myself.

I have listened helplessly as doctors talked over me – as if I were a dummy, a corpse – about the falling heart rate of the unborn child inside me. I have contracted and pushed and I have failed at contracting and pushing, and I have been rushed into the theatre and had my bikini line shaved by a stranger wielding a blunt razor, before being slashed like a sack of rice from hip bone to hip bone. And all of that I could deal with. All of that I didn't give a fig about – really, honestly, it bothered me not one jot – because at the end of it there was her. My glorious, healthy firstborn child.

But this?

This is just the pits.

I hadn't expected the first few days of motherhood to be fluffy clouds and rainbows, but nor had I counted on them being like a torture scene in *Homeland*. Currently, there is one woman roughly manhandling my left nipple, and another trying to shove my screaming baby's mouth on to it. The baby is not interested. Actually, she is more than not interested. She is absolutely *appalled*. Every time one of my nipples comes anywhere near her face, she howls in horror. She is the first person ever to turn away from my boobs in disgust, I think glumly. My boyfriend (now husband) stands in the corner of the room. He looks concerned but helpless. The nurses decide he should be helpless no more. 'Come over here,' they say to him, flopping my breasts back down on to my still-bloated stomach. (My boobs have always been huge, but right now they are mega. They are more than mega. They are *obscene*.) 'You can have a go at getting the nipples in better shape.'

'WHAT?' I shriek, protectively clutching my boobs to my chest.

'He can help by putting this plastic contraption over your nipples,' she says, holding up a piece of equipment that looks disturbingly like a giant syringe. 'It creates a vacuum effect which stops your nipples from being flat. Then maybe the baby will be able to latch.'

He grabs the boob syringe eagerly. Perhaps a little too eagerly. He comes and sits on the side of the bed. 'It's good to be able to get involved,' he says, keenly, as if he were a boy scout on an activity day and not a bloke who has just watched his beloved get ripped apart in an operating theatre.

'Does he really have to do this?' I ask.

'It's all for the good of the baby!' beams another nurse, who is bouncing my starving daughter up and down in an attempt to stop her crying.

'Wow, look at this!' exclaims my husband, pushing the syringe up and down. 'Right, let me at them.' I turn away as he attempts to pull my nipples out. It is like someone pinching you continuously. It is what I imagine it is like to take part in a really, really perverted S&M game, only in a sterile NHS hospital room and not a sex dungeon. 'That's amazing!' says my husband in delight. He is looking at my nipple which now stands proud and erect as opposed to the other one, which has just sort of shrunk into my breast. A nurse tries to shove my baby on. She refuses. They try again. She refuses. 'Perhaps try with the other boob,' suggests someone (by now, I have lost track of all the different people who have molested my tits, and it isn't even 11am). We try with the other boob. She refuses. And on this goes for what seems like an eternity: my boyfriend torturing me, my baby refusing me, my heart just a little bit broken.

I have always been ashamed of my breasts. They appeared out of nowhere before I had even got to secondary school, two great big mounds of flesh that seemed to ask boys to tease me. At twelve I became aware of men on the street staring at them, and by thirteen I had become too painfully embarrassed to walk past building sites. I wasn't beautiful, just normal, boring, average, so the attention was not flattering or pleasing; I knew that it was only because of my boobs. Boys didn't look me in the eye, and they couldn't refer to me without also mentioning the size of my bra (which by fifteen was a 32H). While other girls were described as 'cool' or 'awesome' or 'totally fit', I was just described as a giant pair of boobs. And before you ask – yes, it did get on my tits. I remember a boy called Andrew, announcing in front of everyone: 'Imagine if Bryony ever got pregnant, how HUGE her boobs would get!' It was mortifying, but it was also the first hint I had that maybe, just maybe, these great big lumps of flesh might one day turn out to be quite useful.

In the meantime, I bought bras that promised to minimise my boobs, and when that didn't work I took to flattening them myself by wearing secret support vests, the hope being that the Lycra would push them away. By 21 I was convinced my breasts were sagging – ha! – and by

24 I had changed tack altogether when it came to dressing them. Instead of trying to hide my boobs, I was going to try to be proud of them. I was going to stick them in push-up bras and wear low-cut tops and show everyone what I had. But this just led to half a decade of promiscuity and the nickname 'Breasts', which hardly did wonders for my self-esteem.

So my whole post-adolescent life had been defined by my boobs, and when I discovered that I was growing a new life with my then-boyfriend (now husband), Harry, I hoped that they might come to define me in a different way. As my pregnancy developed, so did my breasts, until they were a ginormous 36JJ and the only places I could get bras from were scaffolding companies. My boobs were clearly made for breastfeeding, I thought. I was going to be the goddamn *Queen* of breastfeeding. I was going to be so good at it that I would be able to feed every baby in the hospital, if need be. I was going to be so amazing at it that I would be one of those weirdo women who was still feeding their child at the age of seventeen. With the milk from my boobs, you were going to be able to set up a dairy.

Except that it didn't quite happen that way.

As I lay in that hospital bed, I felt complete shock. How could it be so difficult to breastfeed? Why had nobody told me? I guessed because of the government's obsession with getting everyone to breastfeed until their children are six months old – tell people it doesn't actually come naturally, and you might put them off ever trying in the first place. But as I desperately tried to shove my hungry, miserable child onto my nipple, I wished there had been some warning. If I had just known, then maybe I wouldn't be feeling like such a complete and utter failure. But it was too late for that. Now the only thing that mattered was getting some food into my baby. But how were we going to do that?

A word sat in the air, waiting for someone to say it: formula. Nobody did. Not the nurses, who in the quest to get me breastfeeding would rather my baby starved, and not me, who thought that it was made by evil companies who poisoned people in the Third World. My baby would not have formula, she would not, she would not. SHE. WOULD. NOT. One of the nurses decided that pumping was the way forward. She started to hand-pump my colostrum out, in a process just as painful as the one my other half had carried out just hours earlier. It took forever, but it was worth it, because now at least my child would have some food.

They brought in a hospital-grade pump, and I sat for two hours with my tits attached to it. Out of them, I got the grand total of 50ml. 'You're doing really well!' said someone, the rictus grin on her face telling me she was lying. But I felt better. I was at least getting some milk, and some was better than none. We spent the next day like that: me attached to a machine; the baby screaming every time we tried to get her to take milk the normal way.

Eventually, we were allowed home, and it was here that things went very wrong. Having thought that I would be the best breastfeeder in the world, I had bought only a hand pump. It was almost impossible to get any milk out of it, so my mother had to dash out and spend £200 on a new one. What milk we did get would pour down the baby's face – the teats in the bottles we had bought were simply too fast. Desperate, I dialled the number of a breastfeeding expert that I had been given by a friend. She told me she would come the next day, but in the meantime, we were to give her formula.

I felt sick. 'Really?'

'Yes! By the sounds of things, that baby needs milk NOW.'

So we gave her some formula, and for the first time since she was born, she relaxed. She became calm, content. She guzzled it down and fell asleep. But while she felt calm, I just felt incredible guilt. What had I done? Breastfeeding, I had read, was supposed to increase a baby's intelligence. It would stop them becoming obese and lead to them having long and healthy lives. Had I now condemned her because I had faulty tits?

We went for a walk while the baby slumbered in her formula-induced coma. Sitting outside a café I saw a beautiful woman who looked like Amélie, sipping a cappuccino with one hand and holding her baby to her bosom with the other. It all looked so natural, so effortless, that I burst into tears. When I tried to get my baby to latch on, the size of my breasts meant I was having to hold her like a rugby ball, practically round my back. I was never going to be like that Amélie-alike. I was never going to be the earth mother I had dreamed of.

I started to google phrases like 'women who can't

breastfeed' and discovered that, according to groups like the NCT, this applied to very few females. I felt like a fraud. That night, the baby woke up from her sleep and began to scream with gusto. Writing this now it pains me, but when my husband tried to give her more formula I stopped him. I was so caught up in my own sense of failure, so brainwashed by the Breastapo, that I only wanted her to have my milk. I pumped and pumped into the night like a deranged woman, but still she cried. My husband went behind my back and gave her some formula. I was furious. At 2am, I called the 24-hour midwife team from the hospital. I told her – and it seems mad now, probably because it was – that I thought my daughter was being poisoned by the formula. But what is really bloody bonkers is that she didn't disagree with me. 'You've probably given her too much,' she said. 'Their stomachs are only as big as marbles. You should only be giving her 30ml at most at every feed.'

The lunacy of this statement was completely lost on me, as by this stage I was acting like a lunatic myself. 'WE'VE POISONED HER!' I squealed to my husband. 'WE NEED TO NOT FEED HER FOR A WHILE.' Which meant that by the time the breastfeeding expert showed up later that day, my darling daughter was absolutely starving, and my husband and I were completely deranged.

We told her what had happened, about the call to the midwife and the comment about a baby's stomach being the size of a marble. She was completely horrified. 'Our stomachs are only the size of a fist, but we can still eat more than that,' she said. 'I want you to give her 60 millilitres of formula right now.' We did as we were told. The baby relaxed again as the sweet taste of Aptamil flooded through her system. Calm was restored.

The expert tried to get my daughter to latch on. She just about managed it, but declared that my boobs were so big it would be almost impossible for me to do it myself, 'and so I just wouldn't bother'.

I was astonished.

I wanted to kiss her.

'But she won't get my antibodies!' I said.

'She doesn't need them,' responded the woman, 'because you live in a clean flat in central London and not a hut in central Africa.'

It all became clear then. I wasn't going to breastfeed. I wasn't even going to bother to pump any more. All the so-called advantages – absolutely none of them were worth my baby going hungry. Though breastfeeding is supposed to help you bond with your child, all it had done was drive us apart. Now we could fall in love properly. Now the real fun could begin.

And do you know what? I have never looked back. Our daughter has always been cheerful, happy and a brilliant sleeper, and I am convinced that is in part because she didn't spend the first weeks of her life starving hungry. My husband could pitch in, and he insisted on doing all the night feeds. As he put it: 'If I had just had emergency surgery, you wouldn't expect me to wake up every two hours through the night.'

And were we to do it all again, I wouldn't hesitate in

sticking a bottle of formula in the newborn's gob. Because while breastfeeding is great if you can do it, I don't think the NCT are correct when they say very few women can't. How come our bodies can let us down in all sorts of ways – we can be short-sighted, have asthma, and fail to conceive naturally – and yet for some reason we expect that our breasts will never ever fail? It's madness, and more of us need to realise that, because government targets should never be met at the cost of a woman's mental health.

Of course, there is a happy ending to this tale. And it is that now, I have finally come to love my breasts. My two giant faulty boobs have taught me a valuable lesson. And it is this: when it comes to your baby and your body, you should never let anyone tell you what to do.

1 You can read all the guide books in the world about motherhood, but in the end you need to just relax and trust your maternal instincts.

2 You will start crying and crying about three days after you get home from hospital. You might actually find you miss it just being you and your other half.

This doesn't mean you have postnatal depression – it's the baby blues (but if it goes on for a while, please go and see someone).

3 Don't feel you have to hide away for the first two weeks of your baby's life. Getting out of the house made me feel human again.

4 Babies can be really tedious.

5 You don't need to lose all the baby weight immediately, so don't even think about it.

Working it Out

By Tiffanie Darke

Tiffanie Darke is Creative Content Director of *The Times*, *The Sunday Times* and the *Sun*, and Consulting Editor on *The Sunday Times* 'Style' magazine. She lives in London with her husband, Will and their three children, Sam, Bay and Arty (aged eight, five and two). She would also like to be producing a film, writing a novel, running a charity, sitting on a few boards and having a thrice-weekly personal training session, but, alas, she doesn't have the time.

2007

It's 7.15am when the alarm goes off. I stretch my legs and listen drowsily to the news headlines. Some handsome hunk brings me a cup of tea, strokes my back and heads into the shower. Outside I hear birds singing. Sleepily taking in the radio, in my head I rattle through the day ahead and begin some gentle mental prep – a few meetings (am I prepared? Check that), a lunch (The Wolseley – note to wardrobe), an after-work drink for a PR launch (mmm … need an outfit to take me from day to night), a presentation to the business at 3pm (oh yes, all prepared last night). As

I quietly sip my tea and contemplate my sartorial challenge for the next hour, listening calmly to the news, browsing my emails, I wonder about breakfast. Homemade muesli perhaps? A nutritious green juice I can whizz up? Some almond milk porridge and chia seeds?

Now for getting dressed. The outfits start coming out of the wardrobe. Maybe the red pleated midi skirt with the cashmere grey jumper? I try it on. A little chilly on the legs, perhaps. How about the cropped jacquard trousers with the white shirt, crisply ironed last night? Nice, check it in the mirror, but … no, not really feeling it. I know, the new navy tea dress with the tux jacket. Great. Jewellery? Maybe that necklace. No. The other one? Ah yes, that works. Several pairs of shoes later … yes, the terribly hard to walk in Louboutins – but who cares? I only have to totter to the tube and back.

I stroll into the kitchen for breakfast, followed by a leisurely flick through the headlines online. Pick up the handbag – the tote or the clutch? – check for keys, money, diary, quick stroke of the cat and, yup, I'm set. Bring on the day.

2009

It's 5.45am and the baby is shouting. Please, God, no. I got back to sleep less than two hours ago. Will he go back to sleep if I just lie here? Two minutes later, the shouting is now wailing. I can't leave him. The snoring bulk next to me is not moving. I heave myself out of bed, stagger down the corridor, heave the baby out of the cot and make my way downstairs for the bottle and tea. It is dark, it is cold and my left eyelid is welded shut.

6.30am. Have read *We're Going on A Bear Hunt*, *Dear Zoo*, *Each Peach Pear Plum* and *Goodnight Moon* three times each. I have built a vastly sophisticated Brio train track twice around the living room. I have done two nappies, one of them putrid. I have prised a piece of squished banana out of the rug and carpet-cleaned. I have made baby porridge and spooned it into his mouth and watched as he spat it out all over the floor. I have cleaned the floor. I have offered him his juice cup and he has swiped it out of my hand and hurled it across the kitchen, where it hit the wall, lost its lid and sprayed everything. I am a shell.

7.30am. I am on my third cup of coffee and CBeebies is now on. This is only to buy me five minutes while I attempt a shower.

7.45am. I try to find a matching top and bottom. I fail: the laundry is three days behind. I wonder if I can recycle yesterday's trousers with a new shirt? Can I? I'm going to. There is only one shirt left in my wardrobe anyway. I pull the shampoo bottle from the baby's mouth and bend down to pick up the 189 cotton buds he has just pulled out of the bathroom cupboard and emptied all over the floor. I pick him up and take him downstairs and – he pukes. All down my shirt. I shout. He cries. I run back upstairs to retrieve another top – any top, as long as it's got sleeves – and downstairs there is a crash. I run back to find him sitting in a pile of Rice Krispies and saucepans. I cry. Which is fine, because I haven't had a chance to do my make-up yet.

It's 8.15am and I need to leave. Where is the ****ing nanny? I check my phone; she has texted to say she is running late. I try to listen to the radio to find out what's going on in the world, but the baby is jabbering so loudly I can't hear more than half a sentence at any one time. I try to check Twitter but – epic fail – the baby has now spotted my phone and is screaming loudly for it. I hear the nanny coming in the front door and I cram my feet into something flat I can run in, go to grab my bag and find its contents have been upended all around the living room floor. I give the baby the iPad to make peace and I'm leaving the house just as I remember – my make-up bag. I leave again – wait, my phone. I leave again – argh, my heels for the evening event that I had totally forgotten. I am sooooo late!

Welcome to the world of the working mother. Each morning is a battlefield, strewn with the corpses of infant behaviour, each scar etched out in eye bags underneath each mother's red, drooping, sore eyes. I hardly remember what it was like to enjoy a morning pre-kids – that luxury of time, silence and calm where some mental preparation for the day following eight hours of uninterrupted sleep was the norm. This is now an all-too-distant memory. I've since had three children, and one is still a baby, and so we have all this plus the tyranny of the school run, of unfinished homework, of remembering the PE kit, of lost book bags, of packed lunches, of spelling tests.

The funny thing is that following each morning, no one in the office is meant to be able to tell the difference. You are the same person (ostensibly) as the one who turned up for work before maternity leave. Nobody has any idea what your domestic back story is for that morning, and, most of all, they do not care. I remember being horrified, pre-kids, when my boss (a mum of two) turned up frayed, dishevelled and harried, coffee in hand, and slumped down at her desk declaring: 'Thank God – a rest at last!' I had been in the office for 30 minutes already cracking on with what was the most intense part of my day. How dare she?!

So you can't make the mistake of thinking you can share the morning's 5am start, the poo, the puke, the Rice Krispies, the nanny, the dirty laundry with anyone. You have to look like everything is just fine. And although YSL Touche Éclat is good, it is not a miracle worker. (And anyway, it relies on you being able to find 30 seconds in your schedule to actually apply it. Spare time? Nah – doesn't happen.) You will, of course, look ten years older, although perhaps there has only been an intervening period of, say, two years. You will actually *feel* about twenty years older.

If I had known before I had a baby what my mornings would have involved post-children … well, let's just say it would have made for a very powerful contraceptive. Because your working life, for many women, stays the same. You are still expected to manage the same workload, think just as sharply and turn up for after-hours meetings and receptions, despite the fact you have had roughly a third of the sleep, and have already performed what seems like a full day's work at home before you even arrive in the office.

By lunchtime your eyesight will be flickering because you are so tired. At times I have even started hallucinating (nothing would induce my first baby to sleep). But most of all, my job in the fashion industry demanded I look like the fashion-fluent, glamorous and polished editor everybody expected. Glamorous? Polished?! Did they know what effluents I dealt with each morning? And simply negotiating a waistband that would close around a post-pregnancy tummy seemed hard enough, let alone pulling off that season's 7/8 trouser length with exactly the right mid-heel.

Great waves of confidence-battering misgivings, nauseous sweeps of nervousness and fatigue, and physical, emotional and mental exhaustion, such as I had never experienced before, were my companions during those first few months back at work after each child. Maternity leave, if you are lucky enough to get it, does a wonderful job of giving you space to reconcile yourself to motherhood, of learning the skills that go with the role and understanding how it is going to shape your personality, your relationships, your values and your priorities. But it does little to help you work out how you are going to marry this new dimension with your professional life. That, more often than not, has to be done on the job.

But I am here to tell you: the confusion passes. Just hold your nerve, try not to batter your child or your colleagues, and you will make it. You are a resourceful woman and, as each day and each challenge seems to get bigger and more daunting, so does your capacity to overcome it. I never thought I could survive on so little sleep, but you know what? I could. Once you have done a full day in the office on less than an hour's sleep, somehow the fear melts away. The panic of sleep deprivation eases – you can do it. Not sleeping will not defeat you. And so you get stronger. Every now and then you will catch someone's eye and they will look straight into you, ask you how old your baby is and give you a sympathetic nod. There are millions of women out there who have done it before you. And we have your back.

The biggest thing for me was the confidence – and in fashion that manifested itself very clearly in how I dressed. After my second child I returned to work and my slim, pretty 23-year-old PA dressed a hundred times better than me. She looked amazing – I looked a wreck. It unnerved me, and made me feel very inadequate and disassociated from the professional life that had once been so familiar to me. What I had to learn was that I was no longer the young fashionling, able to take on every new trend and showcase it to perfection. In fact I had graduated to something more senior, more, ahem, 'classic', shall we say. Yes, that made me feel older, but there can be grace in that (I hope). I wore black for a year, but sometimes one just needs the camouflage. Then I began to put together a wardrobe that was as much practical as anything else – where things worked together at a moment's notice, and were not in any way 'body con' (Satan's work) or 'difficult'. That included a pair of smart brogues (you can run in those), a boyfriend jacket (slouchy, you can throw it on just before you leave the house), a good pair of cropped trousers (pleat-fronted, flattering on the bottom), and a trick with layering long-sleeved vest tops from American Vintage and James Perse (slightly more expensive than Gap, but so worth it for the cut) – the layering means you can peel one off/add another in cases of dribble/puke/breakfast spray.

Those sartorial building blocks helped me emotionally. Once I felt OK with my appearance, I could begin to tackle my confidence. I didn't try to say anything too loudly or try to be noticed too much. By the time I went back to work after my third child I recognised the loss of confidence for what it was: a natural transition phase that does pass. I just rode it out and, sure enough, a few months later my confidence was back.

Two years later – eight years on from the birth of my first child – the magnitude of the task of parenting is becoming clear. What is apparent is that the heavy physical heave of those first few baby/toddler years is replaced by a much more complex emotional support act. In a two-parent working family, you need to employ someone else to do the school run, to ferry the kids to and from their various after-school clubs and play dates, to make the snacks – but you still need to be available to discuss friendship groups, what they are learning in the term topic, the comparative merits of Luke Skywalker and Han Solo and whether penguins actually know if they are penguins or not. I'm a long way from that leisured girl who used to lie in bed of a morning checking her social media feed as she mentally checked through her outfits for the day and mixed her own muesli. But hey, this new me has a lot more love – and light – in her life.

1 Guilt is a wasted emotion. Forget it – nobody benefits from a guilty mother. Write that emotion right out of your life.

2 The Obamas were right about date night.

3 Hummus is a core staple.

4 Tesco's own-brand nappies are the best.

Motherhood: The Memo

By Rachel Johnson

Rachel Johnson is a writer and columnist for the *Mail on Sunday*. She lives in London with her husband, Ivo Dawnay, and their three kidult children.

A note on nomenclature before we begin. I can't stand the word 'mum', except when my children use it with me.

It is the three-letter word obstetric consultants use to reduce pregnant or post-partum females to the status of milk-cows, or newswires use to make headlines shorter, as in 'Bodies of Kids Found in Lowestoft Mum Death'.

Somehow, 'mum' signals the end of having a life and a self, and the beginning of an existence in which you are defined by your children (or as midwives call your child, 'baby') instead.

And you spend whole days with women who actually describe themselves for the first time as 'Freddy's Mum', and fail to tell you their own name, as if that no longer matters.

So I dedicate this wholly irrelevant chapter to the *mothers*, rather than mums, who come after me (I started in 1993 and my oldest is now 21). You won't agree with most of it. I don't even want you to.

Before we get down to it, the first thing to say is this: I know, I know. Your terrible, ongoing crisis about work and identity. But I can't help here. This is your funeral. The cross you have to bear on your own. Because not only do men not care, most working women don't really care, either, whether you work or don't work. Only you care, and your partner and children.

I've been a full-time working mother, a stay-at-home working mother, a part-timer, a full-time employee and a freelancer, and I can tell you this: people in offices are having a better time than the 'just a mum' at home. And the people in offices, of both sexes, know this. They are aware and pathetically grateful that there are still women prepared to do the other thing, the heavy lifting. They know it's the women who stay at home to care for their children who are the ones with balls of steel, not the CEOs writing books about leaning in or running investment banks with nine kids at home. The SAHMs are the stormtroopers of our sex.

I've been called bossy and pushy all my life, and I know for a fact that there is no way I could possibly spend my weekday in soft-play areas drinking Nescafé or going to Tumble-Tots because it is brain-scramblingly boring and shatteringly exhausting, usually by 8am on a Saturday morning. I couldn't do that knowing that that is all I had to do all week, not for all the love in the world.

As Alison Wolf, author of *The XX Factor*, points out:

'For the feminist, unpaid home-based activity is labour performed under the lash of patriarchy. For the economist, unpaid work does not contribute to GNP and so does not exist.' As my friend Janice Turner of *The Times* points out (and I am using her words here as I cannot improve on them): 'Domesticity is thankless, repetitive and boring: careers can be fun. Frankly, if housekeeping and childcare are so fulfilling, why aren't men fighting us to do a greater share?'

There's no doubt in my mind that the reason men spend all their time working is obvious: as Noël Coward once said, work is more fun than fun. But let's refine that. I'm not suggesting I can improve on Coward, but I'm not convinced Noël ever had to organise a children's tea party with Party Punkz, a Mr Tumble-style entertainer with an unintentionally genitalia-shaped balloon routine.

On that uplifting note, welcome to motherhood, and the trenches. Here's my memo from the other side.

1. Remember what Coward said, that work is fun, and fun – in the sense of social life, holidays, evenings out, dinners, parties, hey-nonny-country-church weddings, 'ha ha ha', etc. – is actually work. Work for women! Ever since I went to my first wedding and realised that a woman, a team of women, had organised everything down to the colour-coded sugar almonds and the grosgrain ribbon on the bridesmaids' slippers and the seating plan and the flowers and the dresses and the invitations and the service, and all the men had to do

was grumble about it for months and merely SHOW UP (the secret to their success at almost all social occasions, let's face it) and pin their buttonholes – it was no wonder Mrs Thatcher found being PM a doddle. The truth is most men would prefer to go on a 3,000-mile sea voyage in the bowels of a container ship to a war zone than take three children under seven to 'Sunday Splash!' at their local municipal swimming pool.

2. Do not worry about any of your children's developmental milestones. It all comes out in the wash. Nobody asks about your degree when you're 30, let alone whether Tiggy passed grade five piano.

3. Do not worry about sending them to the posh private schools as I did when my children were ten. You will do them, and everyone else, a massive favour if you send them to the local state school. If it's a selective grammar or a church school, good for you, well done, but don't make a song and a dance about how they're going to what the Labour Party called a 'bog-standard comp', because they're not.

4. Stop doing so much. Parental involvement is out of control. My father's proudest boast as a parent is not that all his six children went to Oxbridge but that he never, not once, attended a parent-teacher meeting at any one of our schools. Work out who you're doing it for: yourself, the children or the school. And in most cases, stop.

5. Stop giving so much. When I was little, we were given no choices – about what we ate, what we wore, what we did, where we went to school, when we went to bed, etc. I could only choose what to read. We had no stuff apart from clothes and books (many of my son's teenage friends have iPods, iPads, MacBooks, unlimited access to their parents' credit cards, PayPal, eBay and iTunes accounts), so we made our own fun, rather than buying it in Westfield. Also we couldn't watch TV as it was in Flemish (we lived in Belgium, enough said).

6. Trust your children to get it right on their own, without your incessant helicoptering, and be thankful. Don't stalk them on Facebook. Do install parental controls, if only so they can get around them. Don't check their mobiles. They will be rightly furious if you do. My parents provided us with the very basic essentials for survival, then got on with their own lives. Which makes me realise that my parents were brilliant, not for what they did, but more for what they didn't do. If you give plenty of love you don't need to buy them, well, anything really. And if you give them plenty of trust you give them the means to become independent without you anyway.

7. Accept your children for who they are. They will set out, at times, to disappoint you. To grow beards, to throw a Facebook party, to lie, to steal, to have sex in your bed. They have to do this – *you* have to grow up about it, not them.

8. Remember that anyone who has been in work will find early motherhood a tremendous shock. I cannot be revealing any state secrets when I say that the first year in a baby's life is flatteningly brutal. It took me six weeks to leave the house after the caesarean I had with my daughter. I tried every day to get to the chemist on the corner to get something I needed, and every day I failed. In the end I crawled there in the blood-stained nightie I gave birth in (I made that last bit up, but you get the drift). It is boring. It is lonely. It is tear-jerkingly tiring. You can't read the paper, because you have a baby, and you can't talk to your friends, because you have a baby, and then, after a year of baby hell, what happens is this, at least if you're me – you have another. And another. And then – and this is the oddest bit of all – all you want to do is have babies, and smell them, for about ten years until you hit your forties and the testosterone kicks in, and then you want to rule the world instead.

9. You can't control everything. Your house will be a tip and no one else cares but you, certainly not your husband or your children. They are immune, blissfully oblivious to the chaos, the dirt, the strewn trainers, the fast food litter, the overflowing bins, the unwashed dishes, the midden-like bedrooms. I don't know what to say about this. It's unfair. Another cross you have to bear, I'm afraid.

10. Despite all this, and all the whingeing, you will never regret, not for a second, having had children or being a mother. Having children makes you a nicer person. It's such a relief not having to put yourself first anymore, but rather a little person who comes home from school with drawings of you. My heart melted when my son came home from school aged six with a drawing of me saying: 'My mum has yellow hair my mum has small eyes my mum has a big nose I love my mum.' What you have is precious and fleeting. Almost unbearably so. Enjoy it as much as you can, even though it's hard pounding most of the time. Everyone in these pages will probably say the same, and the reason for that is because it's true: you will never know you were capable of such love or self-sacrifice or stamina. As for me, and despite all the above, I'm counting the days till grandchildren. As I say to my three (aged 17, 20 and 21) on a regular basis: 'The patter of tiny feet again is all I have to look forward to.'

1 That it was really, really hard to care about work for years after having children.

2 But when I did work it lifted my spirits immeasurably and made me nicer to be around.

3 That it doesn't matter if you breast- or bottle-feed.

4 That if a baby is screaming in his cot, it could be that his head is stuck in the bars, so it's worth checking, rather than Gina-Fording him and 'leaving baby to settle'.

5 That your husband will forgive you almost anything if you solicit him regularly for sex.

6 That even though you try to be the best mother ever, children will still find the strangest things to hold against you when they're older.

7 That, likewise, children will only remember the few times you don't turn up, never all the many times you do.

8 That Clinton was right when he said that 'being President isn't the hardest job in the world, being a parent is.' This is because you don't love your job to death the way you do your children.

9 That you would throw yourself in the path of a car driven by Jeremy Clarkson to save a hair on any of your children's heads, and also, any of your nephews' and nieces' heads too.

Babies Bounce

By Jenny Colgan

Bestselling novelist Jenny Colgan has published more than twenty novels. She is married to Andrew and has three children, Wallace, nine, Michael-Francis, six, and Delphie, four. She lives in France and London.

If you haven't had your baby yet, none of the following matters, because until it happens to you, you won't believe in it one tiny bit. But just as there's no point in telling a bride she'd have just as much fun in a £200 hired dress as a £2,000 bought one ('true' – every honest bride in the history of the world), there's no point in suggesting something that won't be of the least bit of interest for ages, so, for what it's worth, here is some reassurance:

Whatever you do, whatever route you follow with your baby, it doesn't matter.*

Seriously. I promise.

All-natural drug-free birth? Hooray for you!

Demanding an epidural ten minutes after your first contraction? Hooray for you!

---

* Short of evil

Can't be arsed with the whole process and had a section? Hooray for you!

Horrible blue-light emergency and emergency section while you had to think how you would tell everyone your baby might die? Hooray for you!

Did you get a healthy baby and, whatever the wear and tear on the raggedy bits, a healthy you back at the end of it? Congratulations; that's more than one in ten of our ancestors did. One in ten of every generation who came before our own mothers could expect pregnancy to mean death. A 10 per cent chance of dying with every bump. I imagine that would kick ye olde morning sickness into some perspective. (And actually it's more than one in twenty of our sisters in Afghanistan are managing right now.)

If you get a healthy baby and you don't die, you should be unutterably thankful to be living now, and it doesn't matter a crap how your baby got out here.

But then, once we can stop worrying about dying, we start worrying about all the other shit, like how we got the baby out, and what we do with it next. What are we like? So here is my entirely unscientific guide to navigating the areas that had the most impact on me in those early years.

Breastfeeding

If breastfeeding isn't incredibly painful and awful then it's dead useful. Especially for lazy mothers like me who can't be fagged lugging around a massive fridge. I can't imagine how shit I'd have been at sterilising bottles. But then I think of my sister-in-law, who had a tough time getting her first to latch on, and with utter devotion pumped for six solid months. When the second one came along, with the same feeding problems as the first, she went, 'well, fuck it', and switched straight away. I challenge you to find a difference in attainment between those two perfect children. I have met one rocket scientist and one brain surgeon in my life, and I took the time to ask them both. Yup, both bottle-fed.

Here is all I can say to you about that: if you are already taking the trouble to read a book about raising children, your children are already completely fine. They are loved, and they are cared for. That's all we can do. After that, it's a big smack of genetics and luck. Almost exactly like life, really. I do believe you can absolutely destroy a child if you were so minded, but it's very unlikely you'd do it by accident. The real trick is to have more than one. You totally realise how little effect you actually have on how your offspring turn out when you have a control.

Eating and sleeping

Don't ever make a big deal about mealtimes. Either they finish their supper, or you gently and happily say: 'Oh darling, too tired to eat? No problem – bedtime.' And FOLLOW THROUGH. See that stuff the psychologists say about 'praise them for sniffing a vegetable'? Fuck that, that's total bullshit. Food is food. They don't get praised for finishing their dinner, and they don't get punished for not finishing: it's only dinner.

Don't run to your babies at night-time. If you can give them a minute or so to settle themselves every time they yell, you have a miles better chance of them falling back to sleep; likewise you. Well-slept mummy is a happy family, every time. If you don't believe me, ask a (gorgeous, chic) French *maman* of a five-month-old how much sleep she's getting. She'll find it a strange question: as much as she needs, of course. This is one of these things that's up to you. It won't harm the kid to be stuck to you 24/7; it won't hurt the kid to be in a separate room learning to settle itself; it won't hurt the kid to have a bit of a mix of both because you have to get back to work and couldn't decide whether to be a Gina mum or whatever the latest trendy thinking is. Fuck 'em. It's your baby. I did get them sleeping through the night early because I had to go back to work, but I have one monster, one angel and one basically certifiable idiot, so don't listen to a single thing I say.

Toddlers

Although actually you should listen to me when I say never, ever, ever threaten a punishment and don't follow through. Never forget: toddlers want to fight you, and they have: a) nothing to lose; and b) all fucking day. If you say no, you need to be as 100 per cent intransigent as they are. Otherwise they win, and once they win, they know they can, and you are stuffed till they grow out of that shit at seven, which, seeing as they're going to grow into different shit at eleven seems a tragically short amount of time to enjoy having children. Also, toddlers don't actually want to win, they just want to fight. Hate to say it, but someone has to be the grown-up, and it is totally us.

Even though it may seem harder at the beginning to say

no to screen time, I absolutely 100 per cent promise and swear to you that the less they have, and the more time they spend kicking about on their bums bored out of their heads, the easier they – and you – will have it in the long term, as they learn to use something called their 'inner resources' or even, heaven forfend, books.

Choices

If you want to work, work. If you don't want to work, don't work. If you have to and don't want to, I sympathise, but remember, you're still doing absolutely the very best you can for your family. Likewise, breastfeeding, potty training, child-led weaning, and anything else you can think of.

Try not to get defensive about your choices and dismissive of other people's: all of us are just doing what we can; our absolute best. I hate a swing park with every single fibre of my being and, as far as I'm concerned, you could take all party bags, dinosaurs and Lego and set them on fire, but it doesn't mean I don't love my kids. For some families, doing what they do means homemade quinoa every day and educational museums; for some that means a big family slob-out on the sofa with pizza; but in the end, for your kids, it just means 'home'.

Your baby and your little kids are going to love you whatever you do. Then they're going to be teenagers and hate you whatever you do. Then their genetics are going to kick in and they're going to do whatever they were always going to do to anyway, regardless of you.

And they might win a Nobel Prize and never call you,

or they might work in the fishmonger's down the road and come round for supper every night. But whatever they do, because you are the kind of parent who cares enough to actually take the time out of your incredibly busy life to read parenting books – because you care that much – they're going to be fine. Better than fine. They're going to be brilliant.

With love,
Jenny

1 It all comes out in the wash.

2 It all comes out in the wash.

3 It all comes out in the wash.

4 Buy a smaller buggy.

5 It all comes out in the wash.

Motherhood: 1,001 Nights

By Nicci Gerard

Nicci Gerard is a journalist and author, writing with her husband, Sean French, under the pseudonym Nicci French. Her most recent solo novel is *The Twilight Hour*. Together they have four grown-up children and live in Suffolk.

Six or seven months after my first child was born, already several months pregnant with my second, I called in a sleep consultant. I explained how my son fought going to sleep, how he woke several times each night and for long stretches, how his day began at about 4.30am and how he caught up on sleep at his childminder's. He would drop off in the buggy on the way there and would often be contentedly sleeping when I arrived from work to collect him, so that he was ready and refreshed for our night to come. Questioned by her, I told her that he would only go to sleep if I bent uncomfortably over his cot and stroked his face while he wound his finger round and round a lock of my hair, often for half an hour or an hour; how when he was smaller I used to wake him sometimes – as is quite common with new mothers – just to check that he was still alive; that when he woke in the night I would often lift him out to hold and calm him, and even entertain him; that it seemed beyond me to leave him to cry. His distressed cry was my acute pain (this I knew even then to be absurd and unhealthy). She was a very nice woman and she refused to take any money from me. What I needed to do was too obvious. But this is not an essay about how to get your baby to sleep – I'm the expert on how *not* to do that. It's about what sleeplessness can mean, what it shows you. It's about the importance of boundaries, which I don't have many of, and about letting go, which I have always found painful.

I had four children in less than six years, with a messy divorce, a brief period as a single mother and a giddying new marriage at the midway point. I always worked full-time, sometimes for very long hours. Like almost every mother with tiny children, I was tired to the point where it seeped into everything I did: I looked at the world through hooded, exhausted eyes; talked very slowly or very fast and probably nonsensically; often felt disconnected from the world, moving as if in a haze. I fell asleep at the wheel of the car while the traffic lights changed from red to green to red again. I fell asleep at supper. I fell asleep if I sat in a comfortable chair. I fell asleep halfway through a sentence. I fell asleep when singing my children to sleep – while they stayed beadily awake. Tiredness makes you frail and volatile – I would laugh, weep and go from happy to sad in a single swoop of emotions. I felt unravelled and unpeeled, intensely alive, undefended, joyful, appalled, wrecked and yet powerful. I was aware that other friends were doing it better than me. They had a structure and a rhythm and they had certain rules: they would let their child cry for longer than three seconds; they wouldn't play with them in the middle of the night; they seemed more in control and less chaotically available.

I remember my youngest child climbing into bed with me, putting her arms around me and whispering kindly: 'Mummy, you're a bit of old rope.' It was true, I was a bit of old rope. I remember running through a department store and seeing a haggard, wild-eyed woman blocking my way. I lifted my hand and apologised and she did too, and I realised I was seeing myself in a mirror (at least I was being polite to myself). I remember trying to write a cheque with a tampon and carefully pouring ground coffee into the dishwasher tablet compartment. I remember offering a group of tiny children cigarettes ('crisps' was the word I had intended to come from my mouth) and asking someone who I was meeting for the first time professionally if they would like a condom (I meant a glass of wine, obviously).

For several years, I lived much of my life in a night-time world. It's a strange place, mysterious. Standing at the window with one or other of them in my arms, the house dark and warm and full of sleep behind me and the sky black outside, looking at the stars, the lights of London, or perhaps at the fox that would come to the garden and stare up at us. Pushing a buggy round the streets as dawn broke, in an effort to get him or her back to sleep, with the parks still closed and just a few other fugitive figures also about – the night workers, the early morning office cleaners and a few stray parents like me, ghostly figures pushing their babies up and down, up and down, in the grey half-light. Sitting and talking to my child, telling them things in a whisper: what the world was like and how they were going to be just fine; how night was a time for sleep; how I was there to look after them. Leaning over a child who had woken with night terrors, eyes open but glassy, and face contorted in fear. Taking a child who was sleep-walking (sleep-galloping is a better term) back to bed and sitting beside them until they relapsed into a peaceful slumber. Watching them as they dreamed – what do babies dream of, or tiny children? What makes them cry out? Night-time as some kind of vigil, standing outside closed doors listening, sitting at bedsides waiting, feeling myself to be their protector – as if I needed to stand between them and the world. As if without me they wouldn't be safe.

What's more, I no longer slept deeply myself, tumbling down into the deep waters and thick churning dreams, but lay on the wrinkled surface of sleep – knowing I was asleep and waking at the slightest sound. And this state of hypervigilance continued even after – oh, at last – my four children were all sleeping through the night. You'd have thought I would be able to as well, but I seemed to have lost the knack. I would lie open-eyed, Sean peaceful and warm and dreaming beside me, and play those insane word games that make the brain hiss: things like finding a name for every letter of the alphabet that begins and ends the same. Anna, Bob, Cedric, David, Eve ... don't do it. Or jolting awake at three to endure the small-hour terrors that everyone knows, when trivial problems become engulfing terrors. Or waking at five and getting up to bake cakes – yes, bake. It's what mothers do to make themselves feel they are being motherly; that slow solace of things rising in the oven. Or simply getting up and sitting by the window to watch dawn break. Because sleeping is about letting go, and I couldn't seem to let go. But what did I think would happen if I did?

It is dangerous to think that you are the sole custodian of your child's well-being. If I have any kind of belief, it's that you are responsible for yourself, autonomous – and that in the end, you cure yourself and help yourself and save yourself, and that people you love can accompany you, stand by you and support you, but cannot do the job of being you. I wasn't a worried mother in any obvious way. I let my children take risks and explore their world; we did reckless things together; I wasn't anxious about illnesses or accidents; I liked them breaking free of me. I've always felt that – within the limits of common sense, clearly – it is the things you don't do that cause regret more often than the things you do. But I understand now that I did what many mothers do and failed to properly protect the self's boundaries, which became porous and were breached. I read a terrifying sentence in *The New Yorker* some time ago: 'We are only as happy as our least happy child.' These words are a curse. As a mother, for a long time I felt – though I did not think – that their pain was my pain, that their problems were my problems, and that if I suffered for them then their suffering would be diminished. I think for a child this kind of over-identification can be extremely irritating and burdensome, and for a mother it's a painful trap.

The question is how to extract yourself from this trap, which is made by love and which an intellectual awareness does not necessarily diminish. I've come to believe it is through behaviour, which gradually, with repetition and over time, wears a groove in your mind. You let your baby cry a bit (just a little bit) when it wakes and you tell yourself that you are teaching it the valuable lesson of learning how to sleep (and perhaps whisky and earplugs help). You do not encourage your child to play and have fun in the middle of the night. You do not stand at bedroom doors, like a sentinel on duty. You go out with your partner or your friends, even when the impulse is to stay home. You build little fences around time that is your own time. Selfishness isn't selfish, it's good – for you and for the child. You can't stop yourself from waking in the middle of the night and worrying, but you can tell yourself that this feeling will pass. You can talk to yourself and be stern with yourself and not equate suffering with virtue or over-identification with maternal love. You can worry that your son may have mislaid his passport but do not call him at four in the morning to ask him. You can worry that your daughter hasn't set her alarm on the morning of her university exams, but do not become that alarm yourself. Don't think you know things about your children that they don't know about themselves. Don't believe you are so guilty, so intuitive, so powerful and indispensable. Ridiculous.

One of my cherished activities is walking alone through London. My mobile is turned off; no one knows where I am. I belong, for a short while, only to myself. I have a friend who for many years had every Friday afternoon off work, but she never told her husband or her children. It was her time – three or four hours when she was available to nobody. I wish I'd done that, although at the time I don't think I could have given myself the permission. We should give ourselves permission: to protect not just our defenceless children but ourselves; to have fun; to be carefree, imperfect, forgetful, lazy. Once in a while.

Recently, one of my children gave me a card with the last words of Molly Bloom's famous soliloquy from *Ulysses* on it: '... and yes I said yes I will Yes.' I pinned it up above my desk. But I've said yes often enough. I am in search of a card that will say: 'No no no. I will not.' Not this time. My phone is off the hook.

1 If you have books about childbirth that remind you to take your make-up into the hospital so you can look nice after the bloody event, throw them in the bin.

2 Don't wear dangly earrings: your earlobes will get ripped by small, grabbing hands.

3 Try to stop breastfeeding before your baby has teeth.

4 Don't boast if your child walks or talks early, and don't be anxious if they walk and talk late. It means nothing at all!

5 Be a bit proud of yourself.

6 Read poems out loud in the dead of night.

7 Go to parties and dance.

The Life of Mammals

By Cathy Kelly

Cathy Kelly has published sixteen bestselling books. A former journalist, she lives in Ireland with her husband, John, and their twin sons, Murray and Dylan, who are now eleven – plus three Jack Russells who run the place. She is also an ambassador for UNICEF Ireland with a passionate interest in the rights of children and women worldwide. Her latest book is *It Started With Paris*. For more info, visit cathykelly.com.

Ask me today what my favourite thing in the world is and the answer is simple: being with my husband and sons, possibly snug in front of the fireplace, watching a kids' movie with the boys snuggled up in the middle, or perhaps playing Monopoly, squabbling happily over how much the rent is for Hong Kong because we've lost the card. Watching my sons' faces in the firelight, watching them grow and learn, is pure bliss.

I hate being away from them. My family – Dylan, Murray and John – is my lodestone, my talisman; where they are is where I can close my eyes and breathe deeply. Everything in my life, *everything*, comes second to them.

Eleven years ago, I had no idea I would become this

person. Eleven years ago, I was 36, childless, living with the man who would become my husband and a beautiful golden Labrador, with whom I was besotted. I was a reasonably successful writer. I read five books a week, acres of newsprint and was a classic over-achiever. I went to the gym, worked hard on my stomach muscles and never turned any commission down on the grounds that if I said no now, they might never ask again.

And then I became pregnant. John and I were overjoyed. I imagined a papoose around my waist, baby cheerily accompanying me places, smiling. Life would change, obviously, but I would still be me. Just me with a baby, the television advert version: I would be the tanned, limber mother lying comfortably in bed with her towelling-nappy-clad baby curled up beside her, sleeping gently. That was going to be me, I thought. Except I'd be reading. Obviously.

Now, nobody fed me this version of events. Nobody gave me a book called *Motherhood: the Cute Version*, but it's what I believed. Career women had babies, kept working, and if they were celebrities, they posed for photos with their children and said how wonderful it all was. No, they had no help. Yes, the weight fell off instantly, a few sit-ups and their tummies were as taut as ever. Yes, little Coco had been flying since she was six months old and had never been a moment's trouble on a plane.

This was the version of motherhood I had somehow come to believe. And because our world has changed so much from that of our grandparents, because now, nobody lives in those close communities where an auntie, a sister, a cousin had a succession of babies and everyone was involved, and everyone knew the truth, I had no reason to doubt the skewed modern version. As an adult, I had changed one nappy and had had to kneel on a double bed, attempting to use my knees as buffers to stop the poor child from wriggling near the edge. This was all I knew.

I was about two months pregnant when I began to bleed. John and I drove frantically late at night to the hospital to be told there was nothing to be done. No magic to stop a miscarriage if that's what it was. Mother Nature was in charge and She had her own rules.

Early the next morning, I was back for a scan in the early pregnancy unit. Ashen from no sleep, I waited with a line of young girls and twenty-somethings in a yellow corridor of the old Victorian hospital. I held onto my belly, willing the baby to stay in there. But I was old in baby terms. Elderly primigravida, they call us. Some of the girls waiting with me were teenagers in pyjamas.

They'd have their babies, I figured. Teenagers who possibly didn't want them yet got to have babies. I, however, was over the magic fertility age of 35. And I decided that I, with my shrivelled, old-lady ovaries, wouldn't. I'd had my weeks of thinking I was going to be an earth mother and now it was over. I'd gone from virgin to crone with no time for mother in between.

When it was my turn to hoist myself onto the high bed, to feel the ultrasound probe inside me, I tried not to stare at the screen because I knew what was there: nothing.

'There are two heartbeats,' the sonographer said into the silence of me holding my breath. 'Twins.'

I still don't think I breathed as she showed me two tiny heartbeats on the screen.

'I can give you a printout if you want ...'

'Yes!' I said. Proof on paper.

I was overjoyed again. Twins, two babies.

'Twins,' John said. 'Twins?' We were absolutely astonished.

Yet absolutely terrified too. That morning in the hospital, I felt the darker side of childbearing – what you'd been given could just as easily be taken away. For the entire remainder of my pregnancy, I felt that ripple of fear that something would go wrong and I would never feel my babies in my arms. It was always there, always.

Twins seemed to worry other people too. Twice, I was told of twin births where one twin wasn't delivered alive. Even now, writing that, I feel the words have a strange voodoo power, as if they can touch the real world. It never occurred to me to wonder what sort of idiot would tell a woman expecting twins such a story. But with pregnancy hormones raging inside me, all reason was out of the window. So I continued my pregnancy with a wild combination of joy and fear of something going wrong.

I went into a pregnancy shop when I had not even the tiniest baby bump just to try on clothes and use their pretend pregnancy cushion under the stretchy tops. I wanted to buy the cushion, not the clothes. I longed for the obvious proof of my pregnancy, not realising that when you're having two babies, the obvious proof comes soon enough.

I read every book there was, which has always been my solution to all problems. Know everything. The babies were peas, kidney beans, oranges. Their brains were developing, their bones. Watch out for mercury in salmon. Soft cheese. Hair dye, fake tan.

My sister sent me an American book about nutrition for multiple pregnancies. Good food was vital, said the book, but so were muffins, full-fat milk and ice cream. I, who hadn't eaten a sweet for years, ate buns, ice cream and muffins. I followed the diet religiously, resting when it said I should, eating when it advised. I would do everything in my power to make my babies healthy.

My belly grew till I was a small person with a giant beach ball attached to the front. I discovered that being five foot isn't the ideal height to carry around twins. The nerves in my lower back screamed in pain, but I was afraid to take all but the simplest painkillers. When a newspaper carried a report about the harmful effects of paracetamol on unborn babies, I was consumed with anxiety that I had now damaged my babies.

Being an always-informed person is not a plus when you are pregnant. That sliver of pâté I'd had early on, *before I knew*, could that damage them?

Calm came from the oddest source. Lying on a red couch in a red room in our old house with twin babies inside me, I watched David Attenborough's *The Life of Mammals* as avidly as I used to watch *ER*. I was a mammal, I thought with delight, huge belly comfortable when it was supported on the couch. Simply another mammal living its life out on the earth. I was doing something as old as time – bringing new lives into the world.

If echidnas could bring forth life without worrying over pâté, paracetamol and delivery, I could too. Echidnas fascinated me. They're the only mammals that lay eggs. Tiny, vaguely hedgehoggy things; when they feed their young, milk squelches out of their skin rather than emerging from actual nipples. I'd never thought about breastfeeding much before, but watching the echidna baby grab onto a bit of mummy and suck, I thought of my mammal status and decided I'd try.

I was going to be the goddess of motherhood. I might stop dyeing my hair after giving birth (not that I'd been dyeing it anyway during the pregnancy, due to dangerous chemicals which might harm my babies), would forgo make-up, wear coral jewellery and many bracelets, forget my endless diets. I pictured the babies and me lying peacefully in our bed, me reading happily, them snoozing happily beside me. I loved this picture. Unfortunately, it only came to me at rare times. The rest of the time, I was on high alert.

Life went on. I somehow finished a book. Then, my beloved Labrador, Tamsin, my first baby, became so ill that she had to be put to sleep at the age of thirteen. I lay down on the floor and held her while the vet injected her. Some fierce power kept the babies inside me despite my grief. I wanted to keep her body with me, to hug her, not to let her go. She couldn't leave me, not yet.

We moved house in June, a month before my due date. John organised everything. I lay like a whale and directed the removal men from my prone position. Sleep evaded me due to the back pain and the heat. I begged the doctor to do the caesarean early. And afterwards I wondered if what came next was punishment for this selfish request, which he quite rightly refused.

Despite my size, I made it to 38 weeks, term for twins. John and I arrived in the hospital for the scheduled caesarean the doctor had recommended because of my small size and strangely, I felt bizarrely cheated for not having felt a single birth pain. Who feels guilty when they don't have pain? A mother, that's who.

Ready for the new life but hideously, wildly unsuspecting of how different it was going to be, I brought three books into the hospital – two baby manuals and a novel. I was a bit startled at how narrow the hospital bed was. How would the three of us snuggle up in peace while I read?

The caesarean went ahead and Dylan, followed by Murray, came into the world. They seemed so tiny and yet they were big for twins, 6lbs each. I felt the surge of huge pride that I'd eaten the right things, followed the pregnancy diet.

John held them first. I love that photo of him with them, pride on his face, those two darling little faces creased and sleepy. In our small room, their two basinets on either side of my bed, the boys and I were a little unit. I was supposed to stay in bed with my drip attached for 24 hours. But the hospital was busy and I am hopeless at asking for help.

Hours after the operation, I was up, changing nappies. I could do this! Plus, there was expert help outside the door.

I tried breastfeeding and, with the help of lovely nurses, both babies latched on. It was tricky, they might latch off in an instant, but it worked. I will never forget the sheer joy of my babies being nourished by my body. I wanted to cry with joy every time, except when they bit me or when the mastitis was bad. I felt at one with the universe and its creatures: I was a mammal and I could feed my young.

The hospital was noisy, so I was dying to come home where I could sleep, but you must stay in a few days after a caesarean. Finally, after begging the doctor, I was allowed to leave, and as John and I drove home each bounce made my wound ache, and I felt the full-on fear return. How were they letting us home with these tiny beings when I hadn't a clue how to be a mother?

At home. Jesus, the fear.

Maternal love came instinctively, but the courage to believe in that instinct did not. I suddenly realised that I must protect these beautiful new people from the world, but they were so tiny, so little, so fragile. And I felt so unprepared. All the books in the world hadn't prepared me for this.

I had hired a baby nurse but, perversely, didn't want her to do anything. No, I would do it myself. Please go. Another nurse came along: same thing. I sent the paid help away because only I or John or my mother could do it. I trusted only us three.

John was amazing. Gentle with his sons, besotted

with them. But nobody had factored in the exhaustion of two babies waking in the night. Keeping them in our bed seemed good but I was terrified I'd squash them – somebody had, I'd read it. My mother moved in. We all slept in different rooms, taking turns with the babies.

I was still floundering. One baby would finally sleep, the other one would wake up. I knew that sleep deprivation couldn't kill you, but I no longer believed it. I loved them, would kill for them, so why could I not soothe them, why did they wake so often? Why would one drift off to sleep, only for the other one to fracture the silence with a scream as soon as my shattered head had hit the pillow? I must be doing something wrong. Advice to new mothers is like flood water: if there's any breach in the walls at all, it will flood in. Every book and every person had a different view.

If the babies have a routine in the day, they'll have one at night.

Routine? How could you make them have a routine?

Had I been a different sort of person, I might have been stronger. I might not have broken. But I am a person for whom anxiety flows in the veins like blood.

I had spent a lifetime thinking I was doing it wrong. The arrival of my exquisite darling boys, and undoubtedly the surge of twin-pregnancy hormones, hit me like a truck. I knew nothing. Nothing. I must learn it all instantly to protect my sons.

When my milk began to dry up (from pure anxiety and never sleeping) I was bereft and rang the breastfeeding people looking for advice and got the 'you must keep feeding your baby' advice, which was kind but not exactly practical.

I lived in fear of the health nurse coming in case she found me out for not being a proper mother and *doing it all wrong.* She was a lovely woman, but I genuinely feared her arrival, afraid she'd see that I couldn't do this, that I was failing my babies, that someone would need to take them away from me.

But a mask is hard to keep up when you are falling apart inside.

Weight fell off me. I never sat down, could barely eat. I, who had had a lifetime of diets, was losing weight without trying. It didn't make me happy – it made me devastated because it meant my milk dried up completely. I was hollow inside.

At five weeks, I could no longer feed my sons. I fell into a hole. I had failed them. This simple thing that women had being doing for millennia, and I had failed them. I was overwhelmed with grief.

One evening, I sat on a couch and let the tears come, the grief at not being able to do this thing anymore – a thing I hadn't known I even wanted till those hours after my sons' birth. I feared cot death with a powerful dread. I ordered hospital-quality sleep mats which beeped reliably as long as the baby breathed. If the baby stopped breathing, an alarm would ring out. Nobody else I knew had such a thing. But I had to know they were safe. The gentle pings from the baby monitor told me so.

Instead of appreciating their beauty, I worried. I beat a path to the doctor's door.

I look back on those first six months and I want to cry, because I feel as if I missed so much of it. Lost in the misery of thinking I was doing it all wrong. There was no lying in beds with down-skinned babies lying happily beside me. There were snatched hours of sleep and dragging myself up many, many times in the middle of the night. There were tears, endless tears. Mine, not theirs. I cried at anything. I couldn't bear to watch the news: my skin felt as if it was being flayed off when I saw anyone hurt or heard of an accident or murder.

Those victims are somebody's children, I thought. *How could they bear losing them?*

My sons lived in Babygros. None of the lovely clothes people had given us graced their bodies. This was wrong, I knew. Other people dressed their babas up in cute clothes and little shoes. Mine lived in soft white, then off-white things. We rarely left the house. With two babies it was a production to rival an opera at La Scala. This was obviously wrong too.

At three months, they got colic. Two babies screaming from five in the evening. People had advice. Sometimes, one person would hold them and they'd stop. I'd try it and it wouldn't work. I bought bottles of the anti-colic drops and wondered if they had anything in them to calm me.

One afternoon, a very calm American friend with four beautiful children came and folded laundry, which she said was the sort of thing she'd appreciated when her kids were babies. She told me about a friend back home who had twins and a husband who'd worked away. My gentle friend explained how this twin-mommy had nearly gone crazy too. I held onto that information like a jewel. Perhaps this *was* hard, perhaps I wasn't crazy and doing it all wrong.

This was somehow a turning point. Motherhood is hard, exhausting and, at first, it's a marathon.

I began to trust my instincts and everything changed. Finally, after all that pain, I began to believe that I could do this.

Now, I know my sons like nobody else. I am so privileged that I can have a job, a career, and work from home. There are few women with that privilege. The world is not geared up for women with children, as anyone who's ever had to duck a meeting because of a child with a temperature knows.

Career women with children are seen as having taken their eye off the ball. In fact, they are superb multitaskers, but bosses never seem to figure this out.

I have to travel for work and while I love meeting people, love my book family, my heart is shaking inside away from my other family.

When I had to go on a three-week book tour when Dylan and Murray were nearly two, I almost went mad. After each day, I'd sit in my hotel room and cry; being that far from my sons felt unnatural. You are bound to your children by an invisible rope. The rope is wrapped around your heart and the further away from them you are, the tighter it pulls. It didn't matter that they were with their beloved dad, who adored them. I was consumed with pain that I wasn't with them all too.

My greatest happiness on this planet has come from bringing Murray and Dylan into it. Simple. But throw work into the mix and you bring guilt into the picture. Ah yes, guilt. How did I get this far without mentioning it? I take my children to school, pick them up, do their homework and cook them dinner. If I can't due to work and my husband steps in, I feel guilty.

As a working mother, I have always had some sort of help during the week. Nobody live-in since the boys were six months old, but help. Nobody who works the sort of hours and has the intense schedule I do can do it without help. Nobody.

I'm fed up with all the movie stars and company bosses who say they do it all on their own. This just perpetrates the picture of how easy it all is and *why are you out there struggling with it?* It isn't easy. If a child goes to school and mentions their tummy feels weird, and you are about to fly to London, you feel sick all day. Is he a bit anxious because you're going? Is he about to get some deadly disease? You phone seventeen times and look at your phone every four minutes in case you missed a call. When you do ring, after school, everyone sounds happy: *school was great, will you bring us a treat when you get home tonight?* They're fine without me, fine with their dad, but I'm still not fine not being there. My sons have key rings and teddy bears, insane gifts from every city and airport I've ever been to. The guilt presents.

Until I figure out how to not feel that only *I* can do it (which will probably kick in when they're about twenty),

I am going to work at high speed, fit my life around theirs and try to deal with guilt when I have to go away.

I am not the woman I was eleven years ago. Motherhood has changed me the way night changes into day.

Occasionally I sweat the small stuff, but most of the time I don't. As long as my family are happy and healthy, I can cope with most else. They are my life.

THINGS I wish I'd Known

1 There's no such thing as being a perfect mother. All you can do is your best on any given day.

2 Good advice from intelligent sources like Steve Biddulph – the author of *Raising Boys* and *Raising Girls* – can be a wonderful tool in your mum arsenal. Having a clue about what's coming next and how to handle it really helps.

3 Learn how to say no. Women can be bad at it. Every kid in their class probably does *not* have an Apollo space rocket.

4 At night, remind yourself of the great things you did with your children that day – not the bits where you think you messed up. Gratitude helps with life and gratitude over your children – the bit where they smiled at you rather than the bit where you all fought – will reinforce the gratitude.

5 Save some time for you. Time poverty erodes most 'me' time and guilt over what you think you're doing wrong means you erode the rest of it. Even fifteen minutes on your own allows you to recharge. Remind yourself that it's harder to be a good mother when you're existing on one, stretched-out nerve.

Motherhood: The Eternal Imprint

By Clover Stroud

Clover Stroud is a writer who lives in Oxford with her husband, Pete, and four children: Jimmy, fourteen, Dolly, eleven, Evangeline, two, and Dashiel, one. For more, go to cloverstroud.com.

Nothing about motherhood works out like you think it's going to. That's not to say it *doesn't* work out. It does, probably better than you could have dreamed, but just not in the way you imagined. But life, of course, is full of surprises, and in my experience motherhood – at least so far – is the greatest surprise of all.

There are fourteen years between my youngest and eldest children. I didn't plan to spread them out like that, but even if I had, that plan would probably have changed. Motherhood is a bit like opening a huge, endless parcel with your name all over it. The contents are always astonishing: from the extraordinary, agonising, elevating experience of labour to the exhaustion and utter wonder of bringing up a toddler, to the delight which envelopes you when you realise that toddler has turned into a teenager, who you can share proper jokes with and whose wisdom and capacity for love disarm you when you're least expecting it.

I've known, since I was very small, that I wanted to be a mother more than anything else in the world. I was one of those little girls who always had a plastic dolly under her arm. I'm the youngest of five children, and was painfully envious of friends who had baby siblings at home, as I was always going to be Mum's last child. When I was about six, a friend of Mum's gave me a terry-towelling Babygro and a tin of real baby food for my doll, who was improbably named John. I think it was my favourite present, ever. Later, when I grew out of dolls like John and his plastic female twin, Lilly-bell, I'd always be the nine-year-old at the party looking after the toddlers in the next room.

I had my first two children in my twenties, and was pregnant a year after leaving university in circumstances that can vaguely be described as challenging, but which more specifically denoted a fast-unravelling marriage, and no money to at least make that instability a little less alarming. As a result, I was a single mother to a toddler and a newborn by the time I was 27, existing on smatterings of income as a freelance journalist.

I couldn't afford full-time childcare, and anyway I wanted to keep my children as close to me as possible, so I cobbled together a working life, finding pockets of time to write hidden down the back of the radiators or stuffed into a kitchen drawer, always late at night or very early in the morning, when the children were sleeping.

I suppose that it must have been very stressful and very tiring, and I suppose there must have been moments when I was close to despair, but I don't remember them. What I do remember is a sort of magic my two little children and I spun together, a magic glued together, very tightly, with love. Because The Beatles were right: when it comes to your children at least, love really *is* all you need.

And this is almost the first thing that motherhood taught me: there is no 'right' time to have a baby. I know that a lot of friends were deeply concerned, not to say downright horrified, that I had chosen early motherhood over steaming ahead with a career in my early twenties, and while I cannot pretend it was the easiest route I could have chosen, it was, for me, unquestionably the best, most exciting and most beautiful one. Besides, all the financial and emotional planning in the world cannot prepare you for the extraordinary act that is the creation of another life, or what that little life will do to your own. But I believe this: if love is your compass, things will always work out – just not always as you think.

I am a great believer in fate, and I don't think luck just happens: it is up to you to make it. While I've spent quite a lot of time in family planning clinics, I've never actually planned any of my children. I feel intensely lucky – they've all happened to me, like winning the best prize in the world. An older, wiser friend of mine once told me that she thought our children actually chose us, looking down from another world, and pointing out two parents that they want as their own; I like that idea, especially since the ferocious love I harbour for my children has been created by them. They brought it into my life and gave it to me. They are the source of that love and I am lucky enough to share it with them.

Having such an age gap between my youngest and eldest gives me the chance to see all of them spread out before me, almost like one of those posters you sometimes see in a classroom or doctor's surgery illustrating the way a child develops from newborn to adolescent. With a newborn son (Dash), a toddler (Evangeline), an eleven-year-old (Dolly) and my grown-up boy (Jimmy), I feel as if I've almost got a child for every age. And since Jimmy is fourteen, he's on the cusp of adolescence, although not quite there yet. He still ends every phone call with 'love you', but I'm not sure how long that will last. Sometimes, I look back at the little boy he was as a child and I feel a strange, uneasy ache inside. He's gone, that little one, although the sweet, funny, anxious grown-up boy who has taken his place is another version of the small one he was, with yellow candy-floss hair who would squish my face against his when he hugged me, and insist on kissing me close up as he fell asleep for nap-time, smelling faintly of digestive biscuits.

Today, I look at my youngest babies – Evangeline, who shares her older brother's wild physical enthusiasm, and my new son Dash – and then Dolly, their beautiful, extraordinary older sister, and am hit by an urge to stop the clock, to hold them in the moment and not let them grow up, since I know, now, that motherhood is also a series of losses, a series of steps towards letting go, as your children grow away from you. Watching that process is extraordinary, of course, but it's painful, too.

This isn't to say that the joys motherhood brings do not vastly outweigh its poignancy. But I think that acknowledging the spiritual pain of loss which is wrapped up in the experience of being a mother, and mothering, is significant. Far beyond the exhaustion of broken nights, the boredom of wet Sunday afternoons in the park and the monotony of waiting outside a ballet lesson in a draughty community centre on a Friday evening when you'd much rather be at home with a large glass of wine, there is a pain to motherhood which is absolutely inevitable, since it's the process that comes with growing up, growing away, growing older and separation.

Love brings with it loss. That is the only certainty we all really share with one another. I love my children with a ferocity that I often find slightly scary. Sometimes I feel like I want to actually consume them; I'm sure Freud, or Penelope Leach, might have a thing or two to say about this, but I put it down to a desire to keep them with me, to stop them slipping away, however much I enjoy each milestone and each new candle on the birthday cake. The pleasures I get from sitting in Yo! Sushi with my teenage son after a movie as we discuss *Minecraft* or hair gel or what a parent actually is are as rich and intense as the delight I feel at the sight of my toddler coasting around the sitting room, a handbag stuffed with a toothbrush, plastic horse, the stub of three broken crayons and a ripped Beatrix Potter book hooked over her arm. But I can't deny that the idea of them growing up – or moving away and becoming someone else's grown-up love – isn't as painful as it is necessary.

And while no one told me motherhood is so vividly coloured with loss, I suppose I should probably have known, since my relationship with my own mother is one that was characterised by loss. You see, there's a big, gaping piece in my emotional life puzzle I haven't yet mentioned, and it's a grief I've carried into motherhood and which is with me all the time. It's probably the very reason I started my magical, unplanned family so much younger than most of my friends, anyway, and it's all about my own mother. Of course it is.

My mother, Charlotte, or Char, as she was known, had a special talent for living and loving, and she poured love onto my four siblings and myself in huge and unconditional quantities. From the first moments of her swelling body in pregnancy to the singularly sweet smell of her newborn baby's neck, to the joy and challenges of bringing up a large family, motherhood only ever delighted her. Fifteen years separate me from my eldest sister, and as the youngest, I know I held a special place in Mum's affections.

We were, I think, as close as a mother and daughter can be; Mum was even unfazed by my adolescence, since we never experienced the stormy fallings-out and disenchantment that most mothers and daughters go through. More than anything, Mum looked forward to the time I'd have my own children. 'Just imagine, Clover, how much fun we're going to have buying nappies and muslins, when you have your own babies,' she'd say. 'Just think how lovely it will be to push *your* baby around in a pram.'

That never happened. Mum met my children, but she never really knew them. She never held any of them, or spooned pureed banana into their little mouths, or changed a nappy, or watched them coming third in the sack race on sports day, or had them to stay for a night. She never kissed them. When I was sixteen, Mum fell from her horse while riding and was left profoundly mentally and physically disabled. She needed full-time, skilled medical care, and for 22 years lived in a nursing home, incapable of speaking, talking, feeding herself or communicating in any way.

Of course I visited her a lot with each of my children, and very occasionally she'd smile, but most of the time she'd just look at them, then look away, sadder than ever. For 22 years I maintained a broken monologue to her, sitting beside her in her chair as I told her about Jimmy's birth, or Dolly's new pony, or the arrival of their little sister Evangeline. I don't know if she ever understood anything I was saying to her.

I was four months pregnant with my fourth child, Dash, when, in December 2013, I sat beside her bed for a final time. She was 76 when she died. I held her hand and told her I loved her and that nothing would ever change that. I think – I hope – she knew I was there with her. And I hope, somehow, I'll see her again.

Mum's death brought with it a finality, but I'd already learned to mother my own children in her absence, and it's been the hardest thing I've ever done. That pain of being a motherless mother hasn't been dulled by time, either. If anything, it's got more intense with each baby, perhaps because each child has brought me closer to grown-up life myself, and therefore closer, in a sense, to the relationship I might have had with my mother but which I was deprived of due to her accident.

Each time I have held my new baby, a stronger and more powerful sense of the mother she was to me has rushed up to meet me. Cradling a newborn baby to my breast, smiling as he stares up at me with eyes like currants, or stroking the soft fine hair on her perfect little head, has made the presence of the love Mum gave me come rushing back. Each baby I've had has made me feel: 'So this is how she kissed me! And this is how she rocked me, fed me, soothed me, loved me.' And so each baby has brought with it a growing sense of the enormity of her loss in my life, and in that baby's life, too.

I live in Oxford and often see notices on college walls or in the health centre from the Department of Psychology about antenatal care or maternal bonding. Research into birthing experiences, new motherhood and postnatal depression points to the fact that motherhood awakes in a woman a sense of her own childhood, bringing into sudden and bright focus long-forgotten memories of being a baby herself.

After the separation that Mum's accident brought with it, becoming a mother myself brought a sense of her, before she was brain-damaged, rushing back to find me. I struggle to remember the sound of her voice now, but when I hold my babies, or hug my children, or kiss their sleeping faces, I feel she's around me. I have a couple of precious, tiny dresses I wore as a child, and when I dress my children in them I can imagine her having done the same to me, smoothing navy blue tights over little legs, loving me as I love them.

This is painful. Missing her feels like a physical blow that strikes me when I'm least expecting it. Sometimes, when I catch sight of a mother of my age, enjoying her own children in the presence of their grandmother, a jealous green rage descends on me, because I want that mother for myself so badly. I once had to leave a baby group when I saw a woman in her late thirties, like me, standing up to greet her own mother, who had come to look after her granddaughter. 'Granny's here! Give Granny a big kiss, darling,' the woman said, as she hugged her own late-middle-aged mother, bringing a wall of sadness crashing around me, because I would have done anything for that granny to have been my own mother.

But the absence of my own mother has made me think very deeply about our maternal responsibilities as women, and where they lie. Do wooden toys really matter? Does organic food actually make a difference to a baby's development? Do children grow up brighter and happier if they're taken to baby music, Kumon and ballet lessons? And isn't love all we should really be worrying about? Isn't the point of motherhood really about passing on love, in the best way we can?

I really hope I'm passing the same template of love on to my own children that Mum impressed on me. I worry, sometimes, that the poignancy of my own loss has imprinted on my children a little too deeply – they know, for example, I can't get through *The Velveteen Rabbit* Mum used to read to me without my voice going a bit broken and strained as I hold back the tears, and that sometimes I'll urge them, perhaps a little too emphatically, to remember a certain moment, since it's the little moments – undivided love when you come in from work, cooking pasta as they do their homework, making time to spend time with them alone, even if it's just to run to the supermarket – I miss most of all with my own mother.

I doubt I share my mother's talent for motherhood – she was a true master of the art – and we mother in a slightly different way. Mum never had a career, or even a job. I love my children so much it hurts, but my own identity as a woman is also bound up with who I am as a person beyond them and beyond being a mother. And because of her accident, my experience of motherhood is inextricably coloured with loss, too. But I like to think that this helps me grasp the magic of motherhood even harder, hungrily devouring those moments as my children flitter further away from me as they grow up, my love wrapped around them always.

THINGS I wish I'd Known

1 That within the space of an hour, being a mother can have you on your knees with boredom and exhaustion, then, moments later, touching heaven with joy and fulfilment.

2 That it will be difficult to wear black stylishly for about three years after your baby is born.

3 That if you feel broken open following the birth of your baby, you shouldn't feel scared or surprised. This is what motherhood often feels like.

4 That later on you'll regret the time you wasted flicking through Facebook when your toddler was tugging at your arm for attention.

5 That quite often you will want to scream with boredom when you find yourself picking up tiny little bits of food from the kitchen floor and pouring mini beakers of water, but that it will pass, and then you might miss it.

6 That there's no scent in the world that smells better than the smell of your new baby's neck.

7 That sometimes you'll love your children so hard, you might feel like you want to actually eat them up.

8 That a 45-minute flight to Edinburgh with an energetic toddler can seem like a long-haul flight across the world.

9 There is nothing – nothing – sweeter than the sight of your new baby in a hand-knitted cardi.

10 That if you have a daughter, listening to ABBA's 'Slipping Through My Fingers' will definitely make you cry.

Feed Me

By Esther Walker

Esther Walker is a food writer who lives in London with her husband, Giles Coren, and their children, Kitty, four, and Sam, two. Her ebook, *The Bad Mother*, is published by The Friday Project.

I had no idea that I would spend most of my life as a mother feeding my children. When I think about it now, it's obvious. Of course that's what you do. That's all it is really, being a mother – feeding your children and giving them somewhere soft and safe to sleep. Everything else is cosmetic.

It was a horrible shock, the intensity of it. I'm a quitter, I like to give things up if they are hard or boring. The demands of breastfeeding were impossible for me: overwhelming, disastrous. Frightening. As soon as my eldest child, Kitty, cried from hunger following an insufficient breastfeed I smashed open the lid of a box of Aptamil and gratefully put away the uncertainty of supplying her growling, insatiable belly with my own body.

I turned away from any debate about breastfeeding versus formula feeding in disgust. 'It's a choice,' everyone would whine. 'It's your choice.' No. No, it's not. When there's nothing there, there is no choice. You feed it the thing that scientists have come up with that most closely resembles the thing that you cannot give your baby. Milk! What else is there for them to eat? Weetabix? No.

Even the formula feeds stunned me, both with their regularity and their paucity. Can she survive on that? Four bottles a day, every day for months? The clockwork nature of the feeds drove me slightly insane with the *Groundhog Day*-ness of it all – the having to be somewhere, with the bottle, sitting down, concentrating. But there was no other way that I could see to do it. If she eats this much during the day, at the right times, she will sleep all night. And she has to sleep all night.

And then weaning. Oh God! Weaning! I feel sad for myself and for Kitty when I think about how clumsily I approached it. I was still so overwrought, confused, tired and strung out by the time Kitty reached weaning age that the thought of fussing about during Kitty's precious nap-times with an assortment of vegetable purees, which she may or may not eat, made me feel quite ill.

So I fed her rusks mashed up with milk and mixed with those fruity Ella's pouches. I often attempted to give her the vegetable pouches, too, but she wasn't that crazy about them. But that is what she ate for weeks and weeks – rusks and milk, Ella's fruity pouches. Nothing really wrong with that, but food you make yourself is lovely, it is delicious. I just couldn't face making it for her because I was too crushed by it all.

Lazy! Lazy and selfish! I wish I could spend an hour with that old me. Shake my shoulders, maybe give me a smart slap with one or two baby food cookbooks.

I also didn't know how much Kitty was supposed to eat. I compared her, endlessly, with other children – often with my sisters' ravenous boys, who would suck down plates of pasta like they were soup, crunching through apples and sandwiches and pints of milk like waste disposal units. I would sit for an hour, coaxing Kitty to eat just one more spoonful of this or that. Please, I would think, please, please just eat this.

What on earth did I feed her? Risotto – I seem to remember a lot of that. Mashed-up stews. When she could chew and swallow and stopped gagging on everything the madness subsided a bit. She ate egg fried rice, pasta, sausages, little cottage pies and then later, for lunch, tiny rectangles of cheese, raw vegetables, pitta bread, hummus. But didn't other children wolf down all manner of fishy horrors, and kale pasta sauces and broccoli? Sometimes Kitty would take a single bite of broccoli and then leave it.

My horror of cliché prevented me, always, from trying to force Kitty to 'eat her greens', but my anxiety about it manifested itself in other, more toxic, ways. I always felt tense at mealtimes. I despaired silently over thrown food, refused green things. I was probably cold and uncommunicative when she didn't gobble everything down in a starving rage.

Then I read a book called *My Child Won't Eat!*, by Spanish nutritionist Carlos Gonzalez, and it changed my life. First of all, it completely re-calibrated my idea of how much, and what, Kitty was eating. The horror stories in the book made me realise that Kitty's diet was entirely fine. She ate a bit of this, a bit of that. Some things she wouldn't touch, but other things she would surprise me by trying. She was not constipated, or underweight, or constantly exhausted or a funny colour. She was thriving and I hadn't even noticed.

Stop making mealtimes a stress! said the book. *Relax! No child will starve itself. Give your child the opportunity to be hungry at mealtimes by not stuffing them – out of anxiety – full of crackers between meals. You say when meals are and what meals are but the child says how much. What matters is that fruit and vegetables are offered, not that they are always eaten.*

After I read the book I felt like I was flying. I felt released from the crushing burden of failing to feed my child the requisite amounts of spinach and kale. I hugged this information to myself. I was released, set free. I felt as relieved as I did when I stopped trying to breastfeed. I fell to my knees, palms turned in supplication to the sky and I gave thanks for this mercy.

With my second child, Sam, born two years and three months after Kitty, I might as well have been a different person. My expectations of my life were so different. I did not – I do not – require several hours to myself to sit on the sofa and stare at the wall in blank horror at what my life has become. Even if I have slept badly the night before, there is too much to do. And I don't mind doing it now. When I had Kitty I couldn't believe how often I was expected to cook. Now I am just so grateful that I've got all the correct stuff – plenty of chopping boards and knives, really sharp speed-peelers, a hand blender. When there is a quiet moment in the house I do not sit and stare, I put on my apron, I start chopping, cooking, blending.

As soon as Sam required weaning I reached for two popular and sensible baby food recipe books and I methodically went through the purees to find ones that he liked. Baby-led weaning was not an option. This boy was starving and I just needed to funnel food into his tummy – milk was not enough. First time around, these books had freaked me out with their fussy little amounts – 40g of this and 120g of that. Now I looked upon them as my saviour. I didn't have to think! Just do what it said.

Then I chopped, cooked and blended, chopped, cooked and blended, chopped, cooked and blended. I bought more storage pots and a special pen to write on the pots what was inside. Then I chopped and cooked and blended. Again, again. Repeat. Again.

And Sam responded, opening his gob for food. More, more, more! He was like a sideshow at a circus. Watch the enormous monster baby eat! Down went another spoonful, and another, and another! All sorts of different permutations of vegetable, a fish one, a chicken one, a beef one, macaroni cheese made with microscopic little flower-shaped pasta bits …

It's nothing I've done to make him such a dustbin, he's just a big boy and hungry all the time. But I do sometimes wonder if I did Kitty a disservice by not approaching her weaning in the same way.

And what of Kitty, who is now three? I write about food for a living, as does my husband. We will both eat pretty much anything and we are fastidious about eating our own greens, even when we don't feel like it. So I feel often that people would very much like, in a *schadenfreude*-ish way, for Kitty to only eat pasta with pesto. Alternatively, they would probably like to be wowed by the bizarre and mature tastes that she has. 'Is she a good eater?' they all ask, poised to devour the answer. 'She is when she's hungry,' I reply. But that really is the very prosaic truth. It is the truth for most children, I suppose. She eats what I would consider to be a totally normal diet for a three-year-old. She has pesto pasta once a week, she eats egg fried rice, a variety of raw veg, fruit, fish fingers, roast chicken, chips, sausages, pitta bread, hummus, cheese, pizza. Every other day she'll take a bite out of some broccoli. You get the idea. Given free rein she would probably snack all day and for her main meals eat cake. On one or two bad days, she has done just this.

Sometimes I still forget, though, that my main function in life now is to feed my children. I was recently roundly shamed at Kitty's nursery for sending her in having not eaten any breakfast. I just wasn't concentrating one morning. 'I really want a biscuit!' she had howled on the walk up the hill. 'No biscuits!' I had screeched. She didn't want a biscuit, she just wanted her breakfast.

Now she has two breakfasts – cereal when she wakes up and then pancakes or eggs just before we set off for nursery. I try to be creative and interesting with her packed lunch and I can't help feeling a bit gloomy whenever it comes back uneaten, though I say nothing. But there is always the next meal to reset the balance. And the next and the next and the next. Because that is the magical thing about children: they will always give you another chance to be the parent they truly deserve.

1 No one is watching you, except you.

2 You don't have to be friends with other mums.

3 It's not a crime to want to escape for a bit.

4 A high fever will not give your kid brain damage.

5 *No one is coming to rescue you.*

Stockholm Syndrome*

By Anna Moore

Anna Moore started her career as feature writer for the newly formed *Big Issue*, becoming Features Editor before moving to *Cosmopolitan*. She now writes for *YOU* magazine, the *Guardian*, *The Times* and *Woman & Home* magazine. She lives in London with her husband, Tony, and daughters Ruby, sixteen, Tara, fourteen, and Orla, nine.

No one is truly prepared for parenthood, so the saying goes. But some are more prepared than others. They are married or at least living together. They have jobs, a home, space for the imagined infant.

When I became pregnant aged 29, I was renting a house with a friend and working my notice at *Cosmopolitan* magazine. My boyfriend and I were planning a trip to Africa on an open ticket. We'd met in Bosnia – where he was an aid worker and I was a journalist – fallen deeply in love and

* 'Stockholm syndrome': An apparently paradoxical psychological phenomenon where hostages develop positive feelings towards their captors. Sometimes explained in evolutionary terms by a phenomenon known as 'capture-bonding'.

formed a vague but romantic plan that combined development work for him, serious journalism for me and marriage in Zanzibar. We'd bought the books, begun the injections, started on malaria pills.

So in practical terms the pregnancy wasn't ideal. But that wasn't the problem; that didn't matter. We were thrilled, exhilarated, intoxicated. Mentally though, I couldn't have had less of a clue. Someone had once described me to a friend as the 'sort of person things happen to' – and in my head, pregnancy was just another of those 'things'. It was another surprise in a life that would always be spontaneous. I thought we'd have our baby then continue as before. Our child would probably be one of those types I'd clocked from time to time when staying in hostels around the world, the ones with 'travelling parents'. ('What an idyllic childhood,' I'd thought. Not that I'd ever spoken to any of them. Never had much interest in kids …) Our child would be truly international, quite possibly a polyglot. Unkempt, androgynous – maybe a little feral. But beautiful and beguiling. We'd probably end up with about three of them.

How had I reached the cusp of 30 so blissfully blinkered? It must have taken a special streak of ignorance, and I now see in my former self a shocking absence of curiosity about babies or parenthood. In my defence, not one of my friends had begun to breed. Not one! (Most weren't even properly paired.)

My eldest brother had become a dad – and his daughter

Sophie was my main inspiration, my guiding light. The first baby in our family, she'd seemed a miracle. (She still does, that feeling never goes.) Trouble is, the family live in Canada, so I saw Sophie in brief, marvellous bursts. A long-lashed, blue-eyed baby of three months, snug in her chair under our Christmas tree, gazing upwards, transfixed by the lights. A toddler with a 1920s bob and denim dungarees bouncing on my mother's bed. The day-in, day-out reality of parenthood? I didn't even wonder.

My pregnancy was easy – I never felt sick and genuinely relished swelling in places I'd never swelled before. Tony and I were immersed in practicalities, preoccupied with things many couples have put in place before conception.

I switched to freelancing for anyone who'd have me, saving for my non-existent maternity fund. Tony enrolled on IT courses. He had no past in it, no passion for it – but he had an aptitude and would soon be supporting a family. We bought a two-up, two-down in a sleepy pocket of London (this was when mortgages were easily obtained and there were affordable properties in 'up and coming' areas). I registered with a GP (despite living in London for eight years, I'd never bothered until now). When I was seven months pregnant, we took a train to Penzance and got married, pulling two witnesses from the street. Our wedding dinner was in a St Ives fish and chip shop. Our photos were from a photo booth.

By the time our daughter was born, I thought we were 'ready'. We had work (though not the kind either of us had aspired towards) and a home (though home ownership had never crossed our minds until impending parenthood). I knew no one in my new neighbourhood, nor did it occur to me that I should. Like many young working people in London, my friends were dotted across town, and I'd never so much as nodded at a 'neighbour'. I didn't join the NCT because I'd been frightened by its politics. (Nothing seemed more gruesome than a natural delivery with no pain relief, and I was crossing my fingers and legs for a caesarean.) I had no community in place, no support network beyond Tony (who'd soon be slogging away in a job he hated). I had no idea of the isolation awaiting.

Our daughter Ruby came into the world, watchful and blinking, on 23 April, St George's Day, Shakespeare's birthday. It was trauma-free – my waters had broken in the early hours and we'd mini-cabbed it over to hospital. (We didn't have a car back then, or believe we'd need one. A few bus rides to Sainsbury's with a baby in tow would soon sort that out.) She was born by caesarean, perfect, plump and serene from the very start. She was weighed, tested, ticked every box, scored every ten, then sat calm and still in her sobbing father's arms while her sobbing mother was stitched back up. Then she latched onto my breast without any assistance.

You couldn't have asked for more. Yet, almost from the start, I felt uneasy. Tony is Irish – he'd grown up around babies – and from birth onwards, he morphed into this alien textbook new dad, beguiled, besotted, tucking his daughter into his shirt while singing her a strange and sickly song which I later learned to be the *Barney* theme tune. (*Barney*?? This man had driven to Russia in a double decker bus. He'd led aid convoys through war-torn towns. We'd once lain side by side beneath a lorry while bullets whistled through the sky. When and why had he ever watched *Barney*?)

He changed every nappy for the first fortnight. He manoeuvred those little limbs in and out of vests and nighties, dipped her in baths, swaddled her in blankets, always talking or singing and delighting while he did it. When Ruby needed a feed, he'd hand her over (at least there was one thing I could do successfully) then take her back when she'd filled up, always laughing at her blissed-out, deep drunk, sleeping self.

Thank God one of us was a natural. Ruby must have felt so safe in his care, would have listened for that voice, could only thrive under all that love. On the one hand, it took the pressure off me – but on the other, it fed a new, gnawing sense of inadequacy and isolation. They were flying, but I was awkward around this bendy, breakable little being. Each time I lifted her, I feared I'd break her neck, dislocate a limb or drop her. Every tiny task required Olympian effort and concentration. 'Talk to her!' I remember Tony saying when I first changed her nappy. (How could I lift limbs, wipe clean AND talk at the same time? And what was I supposed to say? It's not like she could understand!)

I can't claim I felt pressure to be the 'perfect mum', or that I'd modelled myself on those celebrities who breeze out of the Portland swinging newborn twins in a papoose. The truth is probably worse. I'd never looked twice at another mother (celebrity or other) or bothered to form any expectation at all. Now here I was, floppy, flabby, leaking from every orifice – in a world I knew nothing about and didn't much like.

Tony took a fortnight off work, but then it was down to me. My mother stayed over a lot. Friends came with gifts, then skipped back to their own (child-free) lives in far-off corners. I remember one former colleague looking at my little house, my (photo booth) wedding pictures and my very pretty, calm, fat baby girl and saying, quite genuinely: 'Getting pregnant was the best thing that ever happened to you, wasn't it?' I mumbled the affirmative but felt nauseous guilt. It should have been. But that didn't seem true.

From time to time, a study somewhere will find that, on the whole, parents are 'less happy' than non-parents. Each one makes a little splash of surprised headlines but it has always made perfect sense to me. Looking at the requirements for 'happiness', pre-children, I had it in my hands. I enjoyed the moment and never thought too much about the future. I had no dependents, not much material ambition and so, work-wise, did only what I wanted. I saw my friends when I wished for as long or little as I liked. I was true to myself. Hell, I could even take a bath when I got the urge.

As a new mother, chunks of my day were domestic drudgery. I couldn't 'enjoy the moment' when so many of them involved mopping, sweeping, wiping, tidying, shopping, cooking or wondering and worrying about tomorrow. Parents wish their lives away anticipating each milestone (rolling, crawling, walking, reading, smoking) and future-projecting (party planned? holiday booked? university fees covered? As if!).

Well-being also requires a sense of personal control, and for me the early days of parenthood were a dark, desperate, doomed struggle to claw it back. Instead of going with the flow (I'd surely drown), I approached Ruby as a living Rubik's cube. Hours, days, weeks were lost in an obsessive search for the winning formula (if I tried a little more milk at X o'clock, less sleep at Y, a warm bath, a blackout blind, white noise, no noise …). If I could make the right adjustments, tweak her schedule, it would all make sense, the problem would be solved. I'd have a baby who never cried, who drank at convenient slots in sufficient quantities and slept through the night. Somehow, surely, life would be easy again.

I once emailed a psychologist for a journalistic assignment on 'happiness'. I still have her reply. 'Increasing your social contacts will bring you more happiness,' she told me, 'and it would be a good idea to live life authentically, i.e., not to pretend to be that which you are not. Don't try too hard to impress others and avoid constant competitiveness. Feeling "less than" diminishes us and we feel less happy.'

Well, motherhood all but wiped meaningful 'social contact' from my life. I freelanced when Ruby was asleep, and the fact that she was exclusively breastfed made going anywhere at night too stressful – and to be honest, I was too knackered! I met a few local mums with babies but not people I'd ever have come across in my old life. One had a serious coke and clubbing thing going on while the other talked a lot about auras and psychic gifts. I suppose we were all struggling, but were not sufficiently connected to support one another. We killed time in places that had never before featured on my radar – the wallpaper of my days was composed of places within a mile of my home: church halls, parks, libraries, the GP's surgery, the chemist. I felt awkward, not 'authentic', when I was pushing a pram. I was playing a role. Which made me insecure. Which made me competitive (my baby is more verbal/active/interactive than your baby ...), which diminished me and made me feel 'less than'.

This wasn't 'serious' enough to ask for help. I certainly wasn't suicidal. I had no 'frightening intrusive thoughts', I didn't wake drenched with dread, nor ever doubt my love for my daughter. From the moment she arrived, I was helpless with gratitude to Ruby for coming, for being perfect when, as it had turned out, her mother clearly wasn't. I absolutely loved her – but in a frantic, full-on, guilt-stricken, unworthy kind of way.

I didn't feel the way I thought I should – so compensated by refusing any slack or short cut. I rejected formal childcare and built a freelance writing career around Ruby's sleeping schedule. I was there whenever she woke. I talked and sang and read to her and barely put on the TV. If she did watch *Teletubbies*, I'd be with her, rushing in and out of the room with props (if it rained in Teletubby land, I guarantee Ruby would be wearing wellies). I'd be bored and lonely, hours would inch by until Tony walked through the door (always tired after a long commute). Perhaps I thought that even if I didn't feel like a good mother, I could act like one, would still 'be' one. It worked in a way – Ruby thrived, which gave me confidence. But I wouldn't recommend it as a route to happiness.

Tara, our second daughter, was born two months before Ruby turned two. People often assume you must be enjoying parenthood if you decide to have another child – but it's not that simple, is it? Whether you have one, two, three or four, you've crossed the line, you can't go back. Tony and I are both from bigger families and we didn't want an only child. Our globetrotting plans were slipping away. (The idea of travelling across Africa with a toddler now had as much appeal as jumping into shark-infested seas.) Tony's IT career was progressing, and I was managing to combine writing with motherhood. We were getting more sleep, shaking free of the baby shock.

Second time round wasn't such a challenge. I could whip off a nappy as fast as Tony while singing 'Twinkle, Twinkle, Little Star' (never could bring myself to engage with Barney). I could heat Ruby's porridge and feed her with my right arm while Tara slept in my left. I'd say that I started to feel 'happy', to feel 'really good' when Ruby began at our local primary school. Very quickly, I made friends with women I liked a lot, who had similar backgrounds and had been on similar journeys. Even better, they all lived five minutes from my house. We'd dawdle round the park, sit in coffee shops. We gossiped, we laughed a lot, looked after one another's kids, helped each other out. The men got involved. We had joint holidays. Those friendships made such a difference. I began to feel lucky, living in London, but knowing who was in the houses around me. I discovered 'community'. I enjoyed my days.

Our third daughter was born when Ruby was nearly seven and Tara five. This time, it wasn't a case of being 'able to cope'. I relished and cherished the experience. Not a moment was wasted on sorting sleep patterns or meeting milestones. No 'phase' (teething/weaning/tantrums) ever bothered me, as I knew it would pass in a flash and be replaced by another. (From the moment I became a parent, I was constantly warned how fast it all goes, but in the early days, the opposite seemed the case. Days dragged. Now, with two daughters at school already, it had turned out to be true after all.)

Orla was never a puzzle to be solved but a mystery that would unravel in her own good time. I used cloth nappies. From the moment she could sit, we cycled everywhere. I was relaxed, unhurried. Finally, mothering had become second nature and now I'd describe my parenting style as a little lazy. The less I try to control, the happier I feel, so wherever possible, I leave my kids to it. They occupy each other, do their homework by themselves and have the emptiest schedules on the block. I don't compare them to others or feel that anything they do brilliantly or badly is a direct reflection on me.

To bring you up to date. My girls are now six, eleven and thirteen. We live in a bigger house in the same area, and are chained to careers that will meet the mortgage. Tony and I have never been away for even a night without the kids, and family trips are taken in school holidays. We're not moving to Africa. Our children – particularly the oldest – would hate to even leave London. I work during school hours and these days my horizons don't stretch beyond a few streets. No one would ever describe me as the sort of person 'things happen to'. This Christmas, I asked for a bread maker, slippers and the DVDs of *True Detective.* I've surrendered to the opium of family life.

My 29-year-old self would be horrified. The domestic drudge is still here – and has expanded tenfold as our family grows up. But who'd have thought I could derive such pleasure from making cannelloni, watching my children devour it, then clearing the aftermath with just Radio 4 for company? When did sitting with my husband and the latest Netflix offering become all I wanted from a Friday night?

What I hadn't accounted for, couldn't have imagined, was the way love works to fill or kill every other need. I can't wait to hear Ruby's key in the door each day after school. She's sunny and sorted and wise and kind. I feel privileged to know her, let alone be her mum. I took Tara to the cinema the other evening, but missed chunks of the film turned away from the screen, just watching her face. I can't cuddle Orla without feeling the cares of the day seep from my pores. I've got three daughters, a husband I still love and respect, friends nearby, neighbours I know and look out for.

One of them, Tina, an octogenarian from Sierra Leone, sat in my kitchen the other day, sipping tea. She's slow, quite deaf, a person I'd have rushed right past in my previous life. A former midwife, she has been through a lot and seems to know a thing or two. 'I can tell you have such a happy home,' she said, almost from nowhere. It's true. I have. It took a few years to feel it but now I do, please God, let me keep it. You just don't need more.

1 That everything is a 'phase' and everything is 'normal'.

2 That each of those phases – whether it's waking at 5am, or crying when faced with a stranger, or bum shuffling instead of walking, or refusing solids, or anything else – will pass anyway regardless of how much energy you put into 'solving' the problem. (And it will be replaced by

another phase.) Don't bother. Don't solve. Just endure – and enjoy!

3 Don't get so involved in and obsessive about a schedule that you feel the world to be crashing down when it goes wrong or your baby fails to conform. I've met every type of mother now and can tell you categorically that the happiest are those who don't seek to control, don't plan, but go with the flow and act spontaneously; those who don't obsess over every nap and nappy but get on with living.

4 At some point, your baby will roll off the changing mat, fall from the bed or sustain a bang to the head when you rush to open the front door with them in your arms. Your baby will almost certainly be fine. Every mother does it!

5 Many of us feel like morons when we first push a pram.

6 You know that weird sing-song voice you've heard people use when they speak to babies? They really do love it.

7 You can't 'spoil' newborn babies, or cuddle them too much. If your instinct is to pick up and cuddle, do it. And keep doing it, even when they're teenagers!

8 People are not judging you when your baby starts crying in the checkout queue. They are immersed in their own lives – that sound is white noise to everyone else.

9 Find some way of recording milestones and magic moments. You think you'll remember them. You won't. One day your child will ask you all sorts of questions that you won't be able to answer.

10 Make sure your baby's bedroom is thoroughly blacked out from the start.

11 You may feel trapped and encumbered, suddenly unable to leave the house without a small being dangling from a sling. But one day, when those small beings are up and out doing their own thing, leaving you free to get on alone, you'll feel bereft.

I Turned Parenting into a Test (and Scored an F)

By Christina Hopkinson

Christina Hopkinson is an author and journalist. She lives in London with her husband and three children, aged ten, seven and six. Her work has appeared in the *Guardian*, *The Times*, the *Daily Telegraph*, the *Daily Mail* and *Grazia*. She has published four novels including *The A-List Family* and *The Pile of Stuff at the Bottom of the Stairs*, published by Hodder. For more, see www.christinahopkinson.com.

I am competitive, shamefully so. I even brought up this problematic trait as an issue with a therapist, who told me I was making good progress. 'Really?' I said, 'much better than most people? Am I the best at this?' My proudest achievement of the year so far is being on the winning team for the school's PTA quiz night.

There is nothing that I can't turn into a competition and so, when it came to having children, I looked upon it as yet another exam that was to be passed with flying colours.

I don't think I'm alone in seeing life as a series of tests which must be overcome. It all starts at school, where it's well known that girls outperform boys in exams, an achievement gap that is growing each year. The competition is intensified in an all-girls school such as the one I attended. My best friend and I used our sleepovers to rank each pupil in the class in the five categories of looks, musical ability, charm, cleverness and sporting ability. By chance, the two of us would always head the leader boards (which would come as a surprise to anyone who's ever heard me sing).

Like many academically-minded girls, I sailed through life being good at stuff – passing exams, being polite to grown-ups, getting onto the netball team. The last exam I ever failed was a chemistry exam, aged thirteen. I got 24 per cent, and even that I did as part of a competition to see who could write the funniest, most inappropriate answers. I remember a now-famous novelist a couple of years above me sobbing publicly in the school corridors for a whole day when she failed her driving test, her first ever failure, and I recall thinking how this seemed to be a reasonable response to such ignominy.

Dana Breen, in her book *Talking With Mothers*, writes about the prevailing 'hurdle model'. This is when a person prepares to overcome a short-lived challenge or issue, before returning to life as normal. I saw the world of work like this – preparation, event, rest, start again. That presentation or pitch? It's just like GCSEs all over. The job interview, the report, the appraisal: they all fit into the scheme of hurdles to be overcome and judged upon how high you clear them.

So when I got married at 33 and we decided to try for a family, it seemed entirely reasonable to apply the same template that had seen me through the first three decades of my life. I mean, it all starts with a pregnancy *test,* which I aced first month of trying. Oh how smug I was, thinking that my fertility was something I was in control of, when in reality I had just got lucky (a point which was proven to me by subsequent failures to conceive and a miscarriage).

The birth is all too easy to fit into the hurdle model and as a consequence becomes something that most pregnant women obsess over, in lieu of giving any thought to the reality of everything that comes after it. We aim to have a 'successful' birth and then for life to revert to normality. This turns motherhood (an endless and frequently unrewarding job) into a neat pass-or-fail that focuses on the events of just one or two days.

I did what all clever girls do and I joined an expensive NCT class (you see, *class,* it was the nearest thing to being back at school) and I researched. A lot. I bought dozens of books, I read them, I did some perineal massage, I watched endless programmes with people giving birth, where I'd fast-forward the caesareans since I wasn't going to have one of those. My biggest worry was whether there would be an unoccupied birthing pool at my local hospital because I was obviously going to have a water birth.

I found pregnancy easy, something again that I ascribed to some innate ability rather than random good luck. I had no morning sickness and I cycled until my due date, looking like an orange balanced on a knife.

I cringe to look back at how confident I was that I would go into labour on my due date and how, no, I wouldn't be having an epidural, thanks. My due date came and went and then another week, perhaps an early intimation that there were forces beyond my control.

At last, labour started and I went to hospital where the birthing suite was empty and I got my coveted pool, in which I dilated rapidly. What could possibly go wrong?

Well, of course, lots. There was meconium in my waters and my unborn baby's heart rate was up. Soon I was bundled to the more high-tech delivery suites where I was hooked up to a monitor and put on a Syntocinon drip. When an epidural was mentioned I begged for it and even pretended not to be having a contraction when they were putting the needle in as I couldn't wait another minute for its sweet relief.

When fully dilated, I had no ability to push so compensated by making a puffy-cheeked pushing face, but it didn't work. 'We think it's better if we operate,' the registrar said, to which I remember thinking: 'Yes, get it out through my nose if you have to, just get it out.'

My darling firstborn was cut out of me under the bright lights of the operating theatre after full labour, wanton nakedness, inadvertent defecation, a late epidural, failure to push and an emergency caesarean. It was everything I had not wanted, but I didn't care when I looked at my perfect, albeit squashed, boy. I had failed at this birthing business, but he scored perfectly in his Apgar test and I glowed with elation. At this point, I'd like to be able to write that my competitive gene was removed along with the placenta.

But I needed a far more terrible, potentially catastrophic event to take place for that.

We took William home and bathed in the adulation that first-time parents receive, surrounded by people eager to pay homage. With all the flowers and goody bags, it's the nearest I'll ever come to being an Oscar nominee, albeit one with a huge stomach and outsized sanitary pads. A friend without children or a partner came to visit and I actually looked around our new house and at my darling boy and thought: 'How she must envy me. Why, I almost envy myself.'

Looking back with my overly dramatic writer's hat on, I feel that in that moment of hubris, I tempted fate and caused the terrible events of the following weeks. At first it seemed that we could do the job of being good parents. The community midwives seemed to think so and left us alone after a couple of visits, writing in their notes that I was 'breastfeeding beautifully'.

But I wasn't. William wasn't getting any milk and I hadn't realised. The books told me how important it was to breastfeed and even how to do it, but they couldn't tell me how it would feel. It was as if you'd learned to eat by reading instructions about cutting up food with knives and forks and then chewing and swallowing, rather than by actually doing it. So it looked like he was feeding, but he wasn't.

When the midwives came back five days on to examine William, they discovered he'd lost about 25 per cent of his body weight. He was rushed into hospital with neonatal hypernatremia, a condition where a newborn is so dehydrated that the sodium levels in their blood become dangerously high. It can lead to kidney failure, amputation and, in rare cases, death. The paediatrician who examined him paled on hearing the sodium level reading, and the consultant said he was the thinnest baby she'd seen outside Africa. I had given birth to a healthy child and had almost killed him and possibly damaged him forever. I wished the midwives had visited us sooner, but at the same time I knew that my complacency and arrogance had created this situation. My husband is as competitive and omni-competent as I am, and we had both dismissed the idea of taking him to hospital when we'd begun to worry, because we hadn't wanted to be 'those sort of parents' – paranoid and inept.

We had to leave him behind for the first night while they slowly rehydrated him. 'Try not to worry,' they told us, 'we've just got to hope he doesn't have any seizures.' I was fortunately allowed to stay in an anteroom for the rest of his eight-day stay, where I held him naked against my chest and expressed small dribbles of milk using the hospital's industrial breast pump, feeling madder and more absorbed than I'd ever felt before.

My fellow mothers were very different from those in the NCT class. Here they were addled junkies with drug-addicted babies and scared-looking teenagers who didn't speak English. The doctors were more my type, alpha girls who were competent and efficient, but I wasn't one of them.

There I was tortured by thoughts of 'if only' and 'what if'. He had a brain scan and I remember clearly thinking, 'I don't care if there's something wrong with him, I will look after him and we will get through it'. It surprised me since I'd always assumed my perfectionism would extend to offspring and had wondered how those parents of children with impairments or special needs coped or even, shaming as this is to admit, loved their babies.

I wore stained pyjamas for a week and only ventured outside for coffees and milk-producing protein snacks such as chicken and salmon, which I found impossible to swallow. For the first time in my life, I was crossing nothing off a to-do list. Pregnancy hadn't slowed me down, even a caesarean hadn't stopped my manic need to achieve as I bounced around the day after my major abdominal surgery, but being stuck on the special care ward finally did. I was doing nothing, except of course nurturing an underweight baby and belatedly trying to keep him healthy. In the world where I had previously existed, there were no rewards unless they were externally given – the A grade, the promotion, the pay rise. Here there were no prizes for doing things quickly or for being able to quote from books; here acting in the sort of dreamy, bovine way that I abhorred in others was the best way to behave. It was the only way to behave.

The worst thing that had ever happened to me made

me a far better mother. I'm not grading myself in comparison to other mothers, for once, just against the mother I might have been had it not happened. I would still have been congratulating myself and taking credit for his utter gorgeousness, instead of realising that there is so much – almost everything – that is beyond our control.

I wasn't cured of my need to achieve overnight, not after all those years. I still partook in the NCT group's sleeping through the night comparisons (failed that one, with all of my children), and later got far too interested in whose child actually liked Nigella's liver and apricot puree. Looking back, my deranged determination to exclusively breastfeed after such a disastrous start was part of this competitiveness, though I did draw the line at engaging with the woman who boasted of how many millilitres of milk she could express in one session.

But something in me was changed forever by the birth and first few weeks with William. Part of me mourns the loss of the woman who thought she knew it all and if she didn't, knew a book or Google search that did. But almost everything that makes you good at life before children is redundant or even obstructive afterwards, so I had no choice but to embrace the new me. Everyone tells you how being a mother changes you, but I had not realised that it would turn all my competency to incompetency. I had imagined – or would have, if I had stopped long enough to do so – that once my baby was born, I'd be me, just with added patience, love and kindness. The price for not changing immediately turned out to be a high one, though fortunately, as the consultant wrote on our notes at William's six-month review, the only long-term damage was to our confidence as parents.

I'm now eight years and a couple more children on from my horrific start with William. My competitiveness hasn't completely abated, and now that they've gone to primary school there are whole new avenues in which it can emerge. But my early failure has left me with the lesson learned that the best you can really hope to 'achieve' is that your child stays alive. The rest is all them, the innate something that all babies are born with and which makes them each special and winners all.

1 That a baby will come out, one way or the other, and all that business with the antenatal classes, hypnobirthing and pregnancy yoga won't make a lot of difference to the exit. However, a reliable, superfast broadband connection, along with a perfectly edited online supermarket list, is well worth spending hours sorting out before you give birth.

2 That being pregnant is like being a naive tourist in a foreign souk – the traders all see 'gullible mug' tattooed on your forehead. Almost no piece of kit is essential and all of it will have a 25 per cent soon-to-be-parent mark-up just because it's aimed at you. This is particularly true of changing bags, those bangles you're supposed to wear to remind you which breast you should be feeding off, baby bucket baths … oh, the list is endless.

3 You worry before birth about doing something embarrassing during it. Yes, you know the thing I mean. You probably will and you won't care. In fact, you'll never be embarrassed by excrement ever again.

4 That they arrive as their own person. Of course, environment matters, but short of putting them in a white cage, they'll be stimulated by everything around them and their personalities seem to be innate. With a firstborn, you'll take credit for all their qualities and ascribe their faults elsewhere. Once you have a second or third, you realise none of it seems to have anything to do with you or the way that you parent.

5 It's a cliché, but the days go slowly while the years rush by. The minutes will crawl until 7pm, but next time you look at the clock your son has become taller than you and you'll wonder how on earth that happened.

Stiff Upper Labia

By Kathy Lette

Kathy Lette has written twelve bestselling novels, including *Foetal Attraction*, *Mad Cows*, *How to Kill Your Husband*, *To Love, Honour and Betray* and *The Boy Who Fell to Earth*. Her latest, *Courting Trouble*, is soon to be a TV series. Her novels have been published in seventeen languages. She is an ambassador for the National Autism Society, Plan International, and Women and Children First. In 2004 she was The Savoy's Writer in Residence, where a cocktail named after her can still be ordered. Kathy is an autodidact (a word she taught herself) but received an honorary doctorate from Southampton Solent University in 2010. Visit her website at www.kathylette.com and find her on Twitter @KathyLette.

Natural childbirth is a case of stiff upper labia. There's such pressure on women to give birth naturally. Why? You've done drugs all your life – so why stop now? The latest fad is for hypnobirthing. According to a specialist, hypnobirthing 'releases fears' and helps the body 'give birth efficiently and comfortably in the way it is designed to.'

What's that loud noise I hear? Oh, it's just the cacophonous snorting as millions of mothers laugh themselves to death. A great conspiracy of silence exists between women not to tell each other the truth about what it's really like to stretch your vagina the customary five kilometres. We are told not the facts, but the fiction of life.

But take it from me, giving birth is not like 'shitting a watermelon'. It's more like expelling a block of flats, complete with patios, awnings, swimming pools, car parks and gazebo extensions. So, now I'm going to tell you what I wish I'd known before I had a foetal attraction.

First off, forget the beanbags, hypno-water-births and plinky plonky pipe music. It is Stone Age, what happens in that labour ward. It's completely prehistoric. Lying on that birthing table, adoption starts to look like a very attractive alternative. If you were ever in any doubt about the gender of God, you know then that he's a *bloke*.

There is no word for macho for women, but there should be – 'femcho' perhaps, as women can be equally competitive. When I was pregnant with my first child I was determined to join the Earth Mother Mafia and have a drug-free delivery. Having learned my lesson the hard way – 30 hours of agonising labour – the only natural thing about my second birth was that I didn't get time to bikini wax first. I now think of natural childbirth the way I think of natural appendectomy.

My other top tip is that it's imperative to have the man present. My husband kept saying that he didn't want to be there at the birth – but, hey, I didn't want to be there either! If he was there when it went *in*, he should be there when it comes *out*. But be warned. Being male, he'll completely take over. When we attended the childbirth classes and the midwife asked who was having a natural childbirth ALL THE MEN PUT THEIR HANDS UP. Ironic really, as most men would need an epidural to get their ingrown toenails cut. 'Hypochondriac' is surely Greek for 'man'. And if he says he doesn't have hypochondria, well then that's the only disease he doesn't have.

But do have your hubby there, as it's the one time in your life to get anything you've ever, ever wanted, while you're panting and crying and he's begging: 'Darling, what can I do for you?' New car, new carpet, holiday in the Caribbean – they're the pregnancy cravings *I* got.

The only other things you need to know are: 1) Don't have the enema, because pooing on the condescending male obstetrician is the ultimate revenge. (It was actually the highlight of my life.) And 2) When the doctor's stitching up the episiotomy, just ask him to keep on sewing, as you really don't want anything going in or coming out of there ever, ever again.

Of course, all that's a doddle compared to what comes next. I thought I would have a family who made the Waltons look depressed. But nobody told me about the cracked nipples, constipation, mastitis and mountains of haemorrhoids – Edmund Hillary couldn't scale those bastards! And of course, as a mum, you can't escape. Hubby can nip off down the pub for a pint. But you are tethered by the tit. You are a 24-hour catering service. You are Meals on Heels.

Then there's the sleep deprivation and the sex deprivation ... because kids are a contraceptive. Every time you go to make love, the baby wakes up or the toddler toddles in. (I used to think that the term 'weaker sex' referred to the female of the species, but it's actually the kind of sex you have after childbirth.) I do have one very good sex tip for new parents though: Vaseline. On the doorknobs. Sounds painful, but they can't get in!

But really, does any new mum want to have sex? You'll be walking like a saddle-sore John Wayne in a bad B-movie. As if vaginal haemophilia isn't enough, the wings on your sanitary towel will no doubt slip their moorage and adhere to your pubes. With every step you'll give yourself a full bikini wax. Oh well. At least it distracts from the pain of your episiotomy scars. During the slicing of my perineum, the surgeon uttered the worst word possible in the English language: 'Whoops.'

Another thing nobody mentioned to me is that every time the baby cries, your milk automatically squirts through your shirt, making you feel like some escapee from *The Exorcist*. I kept expecting my head to do a 360-degree turn in a blur of lime slime. Which is yet another reason why a new mother's favourite position is the doggy position (where he begs and you just roll over and play dead).

Yes, motherhood really is a case of 'fasten your sanitary belt; we're in for a bumpy ride'. Babies resemble the most selfish, demanding lover you ever had. Always hungry, but won't eat what you cook. Always tired, yet won't sleep. Chucking things all over the house, yet never picking up after himself. Throwing tantrums, yet never saying he's sorry. And possessive! A baby is jealous of other people coming anywhere near you. He hates you being on the phone, and won't even let you go to the loo on your own. All day long he just sits around in his vest, waiting to be amused.

While I adore my kids with a primal passion, the truth is I actually got morning sickness *after* they were born. But even more annoying than the constant crying and endless nappies and lack of sleep is the Yummy Mummy. They grace every magazine cover – Kate Middleton, Victoria Beckham, Beyoncé, Gwyneth Paltrow, Kim Kardashian – all of them straight back into their skinny jeans 3.6 seconds after giving birth. How did Aussie model Rachael Finch show off her four-week-old baby? By posing in a bikini for a women's magazine of course. You can practically see the three-course raisin she had for lunch. And no sooner was baby George ensconced in his Babygro than the focus of the press shifted to analysis of how quickly Kate's figure had 'snapped back'. Well, my body 'snapped back' too – yeah, right. Just in time for the 'Ms Osteoporosis Spinal Curvature 2022' contest. One month after giving birth and my tummy still dangled downwards like a flesh colostomy bag. And *hips*. I'd never had hips before. Two flabby side-cars rode pillion with me everywhere. What I needed were some control-top pantyhose, but for my *whole body*.

Yummy Mummies kept advising me to train my baby to sleep through the night, and diet, so I could 'take control of my life'. But I'd recently had the equivalent of barbecue tongs shoved up my nether regions and a human pulled out – I couldn't even take control of my urine flow.

Every time I looked in the mirror, an alien from the Planet Yuk stared back at me. My misshapen body oozed from a floral jumpsuit I didn't remember buying. For months I wore a grey feeding bra with the aesthetic appeal of an orthopaedic shoe, old maternity knickers which could have doubled as a yacht spinnaker and milk-stained trackie bottoms. Six months after giving birth, it would have been easier to reunite the Serbs and the Croats than the sides of the fly on my jeans.

And yet whenever I turned on the telly it was to see Yummy Mummies swapping avocado puree recipes and enthusing about making their own teething rusks. When Yummy Mummy is not racing her kids off to Tumbler Tots and Aqua Babies, followed by taped French tutorials till tea (the progeny of the Yummy Mummy have a social life you and I can only *dream* of), she simply enjoys sitting at home knitting her own orgasms.

Feeling hopelessly inadequate, we mere mortal mums try to emulate them. But one week of attempting to get your baby to eat her organic tofu puree (which she seems to think is a decorative option; it's like dining with Henry VIII) and you'll want to put your head in the oven.

One particularly bad day, when I was lying in Baby Gym in the foetal position, sobbing, a Yummy Mummy asked me condescendingly if I'd thought about therapy. She was about to whisk her kids off for a photo shoot for *Totler* (the baby version of *Tatler* – legal proof of child abuse in my view). It was then I realised the truth about Yummy Mummies. These Mummies are only Yummy because an army of nannies and housekeepers are doing all their cooking, cleaning and childcare. The way a Yummy Mummy announces the news of her pregnancy to her husband is: 'Darling! We're going to have an au pair!'

These women are only thin because of the secret tummy tuck they had in the labour ward too, an operation so common now it's known as the 'Mummy Tuck'. The only thing supporting your average mother, on the other hand, is her maternity bra.

So, my advice to you, New Mummy, is not to strive to be a Yummy. New mums should lounge back in bed with a slice of cake and recite a new maternal mantra. Firstly, that lactating mothers aren't supposed to skip a meal. You've got to eat *something* ... even if it's only five or six courses per second. And secondly, that leaving your baby to cry for five minutes does *not* mean she'll grow up to write the sequel to *Mommie Dearest*. I mean, Mowgli survived, right?

So, just remember that perfect mothers only exist in American sitcoms. Any mother who says she copes all the time is either lying or taking a *lot* of drugs.

The world is groaning beneath weighty statues of old soldiers and long-forgotten politicians. What I want to see are statues to 'The Unknown Soldier – Mums Who Gave Birth Without An Epidural'. I want an inscription which reads: 'A toddler AND a day job'. I mean, imagine a job description of motherhood –

Hours: constant. Time off: zilch. All food and entertainment supplied by you. Must be good at athletics,

> *home repairs and making mince interesting. No sick pay, no holiday pay, hell, no pay! Unspeakable tedium* (I used to be so bored doing Creative Things with Play-Doh that I could see my plants engaging in photosynthesis. I once grew a yeast infection *as a change of pace*) *and constant anxiety guaranteed* ('If I work full time will he/she become dysfunctional and grow up to collect Nazi memorabilia?').

Would you take this job?

And yet we do. Why? Well, maybe it has something to do with the way you feel a great joy squeeze into your bone marrow whenever your baby smiles at you. And the way your heart flops like a pole-vaulter into a mattress as dreams flicker across your angel's face, soft as sunlight. Or how it feels to kiss those ivory eyelids, the caramel-coloured lashes so long you could positively hike through them. Or perhaps it's the funny way babies wear their four strands of hair combed horizontally over their heads in a fashion favoured by gerontophile newsreaders. Or the way they babble at you, talking in exclamation marks, punctuated with peals of silver laughter. And the way they turn even hardened cynics sentimental. I mean, who could have predicted you'd become the mother version of Cecil B. DeMille, filming every nanosecond of your baby's life for the archives, then immediately viewing the footage. 'Brings back memories, doesn't it?' you whimper, teary-eyed, to your partner. Yep, without doubt, motherhood is the greatest love affair you'll ever have. For life. Unconditionally.

Although, on second thoughts, there are a few conditions:

1. A 'balanced meal' is whatever stays on the spoon en route to baby's mouth.

2. 'Controlled crying' is the art of not shattering into tears when the baby vomits all over your new cashmere jumper.

3. Re. sex – there's only one thing a new mum wants in bed, and that's breakfast.

4. The only response to a baby monitor is to talk into it and say: 'I'm sorry. But the working mother you are trying to reach is temporarily disconnected. Please try again later.'

And so, a quick summation of my top pregnancy advice? Have sex and sleep now, because you never will again. And take every drug you can lay your hands on. Apart from all that, giving birth is the most euphoric and fulfilling day of woman's life.

So, Happy Birth,

Love,
Kathy x

1 You know what they call a woman who uses the rhythm method? A mother. Being pregnant means finally knowing that there is something worse than getting your period – *not getting it*!

2 Childbirth is the most beautiful and moving experience in a woman's life … if your brain frequency is the same as that of a houseplant. To simulate the birth experience, take one car jack, insert in rectum, pump to maximum height, replace with jack hammer. In other words, take the drugs.

3 Mother Nature is a bad midwife. Forget bean bags and water births. Just opt for the full-anaesthetic-elective-caesarean-wake-me-when-it's-over-and-the-make-up-artist's-here approach.

4 Kids are like Ikea appliances – you have no idea how much assembly is required until it's way too late.

5 You'll know you're definitely a few nappies short of a packet of Pampers when you find yourself sitting in the playpen with the baby sitting out of it, giving you one

of those disappointed 'Hey, I gave you the best year of my life!' looks.

6 Don't ever let your kids address you by your Christian name. This is not only nauseatingly trendy, but *way* too informal. I mean, it's not as though you've known each other very long!

7 Working mums juggling kids and career and trying not to drop anything could be in the Moscow State Circus. Just remember that you can have it all, but not all at once.

8 When your progeny annoy you, remember that you have a secret weapon – the home videos of their births, enabling you to replay the agony to your children *on all their significant birthdays*!

9 Two children is enough. Personally, I'm so paranoid about getting pregnant again I've put a condom on my vibrator.

10 But don't worry. You'll be fine. Childbirth is like a Chinese takeaway – you forget it straight afterwards.

On Being an 'Older Mum'

By Lucy Porter

Lucy Porter is an actress, writer and comedian. She lives in London with her husband, Justin Edwards, and their children, Emily, four, and John, three.

I remember very clearly the moment I realised that I wanted to have children. I was 37 years old, 400 miles away from home and sixteen weeks pregnant. I had been doing a gig at The Stand Comedy Club in Edinburgh. I came off stage at the interval and noticed I was bleeding a tiny bit, then at the end of the show I was bleeding a lot. I told the lovely venue manager Kenny, and he rushed me to Edinburgh Royal Infirmary immediately.

Although I'd never have admitted it to anyone then, I was still not 100 per cent certain that I was ready for motherhood. When I had been for my twelve-week scan I thought it was cool to see the foetus, but I was more impressed with the ultrasound technology than my own biology. Intellectually, I appreciated how lucky I was to have got pregnant with relatively few problems, but I still couldn't quite reconcile myself to being a parent. I had decided I'd just ignore my pregnancy and carry on as if nothing were happening.

That night, as the nurse searched for signs of life, I thought about how sad I felt for my husband and our families, and then it hit me how sad I felt for my baby and myself. It seemed to me that I had spent so many years justifying and embracing my decision not to have children that I felt I was betraying a part of me by procreating. But when I heard a heartbeat, I understood that things had changed. I resolved to do everything I could to be the best, most proactive pregnant lady the world had ever known.

Back home in London, I started going to pregnancy yoga and swimming every day. I had hypnotherapy, wrote a detailed birth plan insisting that I wanted no medical interventions and only gas and air for pain relief. I even – and look away now if you're squeamish – did perineal massage. All this to ensure that labour would be stress-free and painless for all concerned.

I ended up having an epidural, ventouse and forceps, and was moments away from a C-section when my daughter finally emerged. I've kept my birth plan to look at when I need a really good laugh. Even when I realised that the hours I'd spent rubbing almond oil into my unmentionables would have been better spent going to the cinema or learning Mandarin, I was so delighted with Emily that I didn't care.

Our first night together in hospital was a bit rough. My husband was sent away so I was left on my own with a tiny, furious stranger. In my head, my life is a sitcom, and I was sure an audience would have found my clumsy attempts to change nappies and fasten Babygro poppers adorable and endearing. But Emily was a tough crowd.

There was some worry that Emily might have a problem with one of her kidneys. We stayed in hospital for a few days so they could do scans and keep an eye on her. The University College of London Hospital was amazing (SAVE THE NHS!) and I will be forever in their debt. In a perfect world, though, I would have gone through my post-birth comedown at home. I was on a thrilling hormonal roller-coaster ride as well as being incredibly concerned about our precious baby, and I kept having to find places to hide for a quick cry. When they told us our daughter was fine and we could take her home, the dam burst and I openly wailed in unison with Emily.

When we finally left the hospital with Emily, my husband and I performed an unintentional but hilarious physical comedy double act with the car seat. The Chuckle Brothers would have killed for that routine, but Emily remained a tough crowd. Once we'd wrangled her in, we drove at five miles per hour all the way home, gingerly carried her upstairs, and then we all sat awkwardly looking at each other for a few hours. We'd spent so much time planning the birth that we hadn't really thought about what to do afterwards! Thank God our friends Margaret and Dan had sent a muffin basket so we could drown our uncertainty in carbs.

My mum was 40 when she had me, and by 1970s standards that was ancient. She had 'GERIATRIC MOTHER' plastered all over her medical notes, and the other women on the maternity ward commiserated with her about her unfortunate accident; the idea that someone her age would have got pregnant on purpose was inconceivable. Pardon the pun. My dad is eight years older, so he was pushing 50 when I made my appearance.

When I started school, it dawned on me that my parents weren't like the other children's. Even before I really knew what 'cool' meant, I realised that my parents were very much not it. Jasmine Fitter's mum and dad owned a video camera and let her eat Pop Tarts for breakfast, whereas my mum and dad had a phonograph and we lived on a wartime diet of salted porridge and lard. My head teacher once praised me in assembly because she'd seen me helping a frail old man cross the road. I had to sit there silently knowing that I'd just been out walking with my dad.

I inwardly resolved not to leave parenthood so late myself, and to that end I moved in with my first serious boyfriend while I was still at university. When all my undergraduate chums were out clubbing and listening to drum and bass, I was at home hearing the approaching peal of wedding bells and patter of tiny feet.

Unfortunately, in my determination to settle down, I'd failed to grasp that it wasn't what I really wanted. I envied my partying friends. Deep down I was adventurous and impulsive, and domesticity was driving me nuts. My boyfriend was sensible, careful and a bit grumpy. It was like Lindsay Lohan trying to make a go of it with Gordon

Brown, and inevitably it ended in tears. Mine, not his – I think he realised he'd had a lucky escape.

Released back into the wild, I made up for lost time. I settled on stand-up comedy as a career, which meant I spent my mid-twenties staying up late and getting drunk with strangers every night. Work took me all over the world, and I adopted poker as a hobby. This allowed me to stay up even later and get even drunker with even stranger strangers in places like Las Vegas. It was an empty, soulless existence, like a permanent stag night, and – yes, of course – I loved every minute of it.

OK, so I hadn't fulfilled my dream of being a young mum, but then I hadn't fulfilled my dream of being the bass player in a successful indie band either, and I was learning to live with that. I decided that motherhood wasn't a necessary ingredient for a happy life.

In fact I made it my mission to spread this message through my stand-up act. I gleefully told audiences that the desire to spawn was no more than an atavistic impulse. Bringing children into the world was environmentally disastrous, financially irresponsible and unforgivably selfish. May I now take a moment to apologise to anyone who came to see my shows during that period – especially if you had booked a babysitter, thinking you'd go out to a comedy night to have a good time?

I was equally adamant that marriage was a pursuit for fantasists and simpletons. Inevitably, what happened next was that I met a man I adored, and badgered him relentlessly until he agreed to marry me. One tipsy night just before our wedding, we both simultaneously confessed that we weren't entirely appalled by the notion of children. Suddenly motherhood was back on the menu, and I felt the first stirrings of broodiness. Suddenly I didn't care about being unforgivably selfish.

Although my heart said go for it, my head was still reluctant. But, at 36, I reassured my reluctant side with the fact that I might not be able to conceive. Every time I saw a newspaper article about a pregnant celebrity, I would desperately scan it for her age. At that time, my specialist subject on Mastermind would have been 'ages at which famous people have had babies': Julianne Moore: 41, Iman: 45, Geena Davies: 48! Embarrassingly, I am writing all these from memory, I don't even need to check them.

The first few months of parenthood we veered from feeling like we were in Guantanamo Bay with one tiny, sadistic guard, to utter, unadulterated bliss. Given how quickly we'd gone from courtship to marriage to parenthood, this was the longest period my husband and I had ever spent together. I'd married him because he was the funniest man I'd ever met, and I have never laughed so much as during our 'babymoon' (ick). Naturally, much of that was hysteria due to sleep deprivation, but we belly laughed, mostly over improvised songs about poo. You had to be there.

After about six weeks, my husband had to go away for a month of filming. Our dreamy days of being a magic three were over, and Emily and I were on our own. Happily there are lots of parks, museums and parent and baby activities near where we live. I relished the baby club screenings every Wednesday at my local cinema, and saw more movies than I had in years. I was so impressed by these, in fact, that I started an infant-friendly comedy club that I am still running to this day (quick plug: www.screamingwith laughter.com).

Although I had given up my life as a touring comedian for the time being, I started doing other bits and bobs of work ridiculously early. I achieved this largely by doing things where I didn't need childcare. About two weeks after Emily was born I was back doing a regular voiceover job for an online PlayStation magazine. I would rock up to the sound studio and hand her over to one of the production team while I went into the recording booth and did my thing. They would hold her up on the mixing desk so she could see me. There was something incredibly refreshing about being in a soundproof box at that time in my life. I also took Emily to a few night-time stand-up shows. I discovered baby-wearing and found it incredibly liberating.

When Emily got to about five months, she started to get into a recognisable routine. I felt I was just coming out of the tunnel and could start to devise a proper schedule for returning to work. In the event, my plans were scuppered by circumstances beyond my (birth) control.

I was pregnant again by the time Emily was six months old. If I'm honest this was a happy accident – planning to have two children under two seems frankly masochistic – but completely welcome. I had my son John a month before my 39th birthday. I was a year younger than my mum was when I was born (in your face, Mum!) and second time around I was much more confident about the whole business.

John was a very easy baby, and because I'd been through it all so recently with Emily, we hardly had to buy anything. I still had all Emily's little outfits. I did grudgingly purchase a couple of more 'masculine' items, but John spent most of his time at home relaxing in ladies' clothing. I'm hoping this will equip him to be a Tory MP later in life.

Now John is two. Both he and Emily go to a brilliant nursery, and I have returned to work properly. I had no idea how hard getting back into my career would be, even though I love my job. My confidence was really dented by the break. Since being a comedian is largely about appearing fearless and nonchalant, it felt a bit like going back to work as a wine taster having lost my sense of smell.

From our experience of parenting so far, my only certainty is that the things we worried and fretted over beforehand have given us little trouble. All our major problems have come from completely unexpected directions, and we couldn't have prepared for them anyway. Certainly, I wish I hadn't spent so much time agonising about being an older parent.

There are loads of advantages to having babies later. Little did I know that my many life experiences would come in handy. All the late nights I'd spent playing poker meant that keeping the crazy hours of a newborn did not faze me. I have fond memories of catching up on missed episodes of *Mad Men* with Emily at three in the morning, and then going back to bed with her after breakfast.

I wasn't that concerned about my social life being curtailed. For a start, I knew the confinement period was limited – over the years I had seen friends disappear from view for about five years and then miraculously resurface when the kids started school. Also, I find early nights and sobriety a lot easier than I would have in my twenties. These days I'd only agree to a date with Ryan Gosling if he promised I'd be back in time for my herbal tea in front of *Newsnight*.

Being older, I think I also care way less what other people think of me. My younger self might have been embarrassed that when people came round to see the new baby they had to step over piles of unwashed clothes and clear takeaway cartons off the sofa in order to sit down. I might have been a bit more reticent about breastfeeding in public. I almost certainly wouldn't have told the world that I'd done perineal massage.

Obviously, there are disadvantages as well. There's no denying that I was not at my physical peak. And if the visible signs of ageing were creeping up before, after childbirth they have positively galloped. Pictures of me pre-babies compared to now look like those before and after photos of crystal meth addicts.

My main worry was how being an older mum would affect my children. I am lucky that right now they still have four doting grandparents who are amazingly youthful, and I hope they get to enjoy each other for as long as possible. I know that I have to try extra hard to stay fit and healthy, to give myself the best chance of being there to help out with my own grandchildren.

Everyone says you appreciate your parents more when you become one yourself. If I can give my kids just a fraction of the love and security I got from my mum and dad I won't have done a bad job.

I wouldn't necessarily encourage my children to leave parenthood as late as I did – selfishly I'd like them to get cracking ASAP – but I have got a bit sick of reading newspaper articles berating women (and less frequently men) for leaving it 'too late'. Especially when a lot of the research about fertility is patchy at best (some research, it turns out, is based on French birth records from 1670 to 1830!).

Like many people, I didn't really choose to delay parenthood, circumstances forced it on me and I was quite keen to find a decent co-parent before I took the plunge. Who cares how old I was when I did it? Who cares how old Mariah Carey was? Or Nicole Kidman? (Both 41, to save you the trip to Wikipedia.)

I think the main lesson that having small children teaches you is that you can never be prepared for it, no matter how old (or young) you are, how many other children you've looked after or how much background reading you've done. The only advice worth having is: please, don't bother with perineal massage.

1 You might have to toughen up your nipples. I totally understand why breastfeeding advocates emphasise how easy breastfeeding can be. Once you're up and running it is awesome, but I found the first few days really difficult. I had my breasts manhandled by dozens of people – I'm not even convinced they were all medical professionals – but no matter how many times someone tried to get the nipple correctly positioned, it always hurt. My salvation literally came in the form of a salve called Lansinoh cream. I slathered it on and it really helped to toughen up my nips.

2 Babies don't take up much room. We live in a very bijou second floor flat with a tiny second bedroom. When we got pregnant lots of people asked us: 'So, when are you moving?' I did panic about lack of space, but we love our little home and decided to sit tight. I'm so glad we did, because I think our confined quarters actually made the early months with both babies so much easier. In the first weeks, it's almost impossible to eat a meal without interruption, but we could have our dinner in the kitchen and quickly pop through to the next room to soothe the baby. Middle of the night trips to the nursery are a lot easier when you don't have to traipse up and down stairs.

The kids have loved sharing a room, and even when one is being really noisy, the other one can sleep through it. I think it has even helped them sleep better. Admittedly, it was pretty hard getting two children up two flights of stairs to our front door when neither of them could walk properly. I had to work out whether it was safer to leave the baby in the hall, then run upstairs with the toddler, lock her into the flat, then run back down for the baby or leave the toddler in the hall and take the baby upstairs … it was like that puzzle about ferrying hens, foxes and bags of grain across a river.

3 Children's TV is surprisingly good. Before I had kids I was determined to limit the amount they watched. Now I try to limit it to 'no more than will actually make their eyes bleed'. I am very impressed with parents who can fill the long, wet winter days with healthy and wholesome activities, but I rely heavily on CBeebies. I also very much like Channel 5's *Milkshake* gang. Just watch that you don't find yourself fancying the presenters. My husband got a bit giddy when one of Nickelodeon's *Go! Go! Go!* girls tweeted him, which was pathetic. Although if Sid from *Let's Play* wants my number …

4 Babies are surprisingly predictable. The most useful book we were given was *Your Baby Week by Week*. Even though we thought we'd given birth to a unique little snowflake, it turns out they all do the same things at roughly the same time in terms of rolling over, holding their heads up, developing weird rashes, etc. Lots of parenting websites send similar weekly and monthly emails for free.

5 It's normal to be obsessed with poo. For the first few months of both my babies' lives I don't think my husband and I had a conversation that didn't contain some reference to excrement. The colour, frequency and consistency of our offspring's stools were fascinating to us, and we were baffled when strangers didn't seem to share our enthusiasm.

The Sleeping Babies Lie

By Alix Walker

When she's not acting as personal assistant, chef and 24-hour entertainer to her one-year-old son, Miller Gray, Alix Walker is Associate Editor of *Stylist* magazine. She lives in Islington with her husband, Matt.

French Children Don't Throw Food was my bible when I was pregnant. I would nod along, circling paragraphs, comforted by the belief that just like those clever French ladies, I too would have a baby who 'slept through' from twelve weeks old. Silly English mothers who leapt every time their baby stirred, they should be using their maternal intuition and setting *boundaries*. My honorary Frenchman would 'self soothe' in his own room like the independent well-rounded child he was made to be.

Fast-forward eight months and my baby sleeps spread-eagled across my bed most nights. I rock and sing and dance him to sleep like a Redcoat at Butlin's. I dart from my bed every time he stirs, and my sheets are damp from discarded milk bottles, sachets of Calpol and drool. I have 'slept' with my head on the bedside table, on a book, on a remote control, on a pool of sick … all in fear of waking my tiny master. My husband, now more like the lodger, moved into the spare room months ago – there is only room for one man in my bed. I sometimes drink wine before noon, and my diet largely consists of fistfuls of Maltesers and coffee. In short, I do what I have to do to get through each day on less sleep than I ever imagined possible.

When you're debating the merits of which Bugaboo to get – the Chameleon versus the Bee – the 'sleepless nights' warnings from friends just seem like background noise. I'm ashamed to admit that I thought they must be doing something wrong and that, guided by French wisdom, my baby would sleep peacefully on demand. I certainly didn't realise that sleep – getting it, delaying it, prolonging it – would become more important to me than breathing. (Incidentally I have spent dangerous periods of time not breathing in case the sound of me exhaling wakes him up.) I had no idea how desperate I'd feel without it (I once walked to the 24-hour garage at 5am just to feel like I wasn't the only person in the world awake).

I spent the first three weeks of my baby's life sleeping on the couch. I'd had a C-section and it was too hard to get in and out of bed, plus I was so terrified of falling asleep while I was feeding that I found it easier to just stay awake. (I watched seven series of *Geordie Shore* before my baby's two-week birthday.) So far, so normal. But a few months later it became clear that my nocturnal life wasn't so normal any more. Suddenly everyone around me started to emerge from the sleepless fog and venture out on date nights or friends' birthdays. They talked of cooking dinner without a baby attached to them, of reading books with *two* hands and watching box sets. I internally wept – we hadn't even eaten dinner on our own yet. As people ticked off their 'firsts' post-baby – hangovers, spa visits, sleepovers with grandparents – I winced. What was I doing wrong?

Everywhere I looked babies were asleep. In cafés, in bookshops, in restaurants, but mine was *always* awake. Weekly meet-ups with my NCT friends became torturous. 'Emma did a six-hour stretch last night'; 'Archie is putting himself back to sleep'; 'I'm worried Gracie sleeps *too* much'. Oh. So your baby doesn't wake up every single hour and only drops off after 90 minutes attached to your boob? You don't sleep upright in bed with them balanced on top of you and a white noise app blaring in your ear? No? No? It turned out that I was on my own here. And so, deranged and bemused, I was lulled into the dark and seedy word of sleep advice.

The baby sleep aid industry is worth billions of pounds, with the average sleep trainer (someone who arrives at your house like Mary Poppins to teach your baby to sleep) costing £1,000 a night. It's no surprise it's such a money-maker when you consider it's built on the premise of selling miracles to desperate women at their weakest hour: right around 3am when, having just thrown a bottle at your partner's sleeping head, you head to Google. Right then, in the dark, it makes *perfect* sense that you should put your baby down awake and they'll fall straight off (they've never fallen asleep without a 90-minute Oscar-worthy performance before, but sure, this time it'll work), so you buy the magic sleep programme. But then you read someone on Mumsnet saying you that you should *never* let your baby nap after 5pm when you could swear the health visitor told you to never wake a sleeping baby, and suddenly your confidence starts to waver. An hour later, having bypassed Gina Ford's method, the arguments for and against feeding on demand, a nasty debate about the cry-it-out method and an essay on why attachment parenting is the future, you finally stumble across the *regressions*. Ah, not to worry, your baby is clearly just going through the four-month regression. But hang on a minute, there's also a five-, six-, seven-, eight- and nine-month regression too. And on and on and on it goes. The advice, the warnings, the lectures all raced around my head like the cruellest tinnitus.

The next day when my latest sleep theory didn't go to plan I would begin the justification process. It was because we had veered from THE ROUTINE. '*Of course* our three-month-old can tell that he had his bath at 6.13pm, not 6pm,' I would shout at my bemused husband. He was definitely overtired. He'd had too much milk. Too little milk. He was teething. Ill. Silent reflux? Constipation? The reality was I was as clueless as the so-called experts. Because no one really knows how to get a baby to sleep through the night. Just like no one knows what colic is or why some people go into labour naturally and some people don't. You only need to see how rapidly the latest advice on everything baby-related changes – it wasn't that long ago that paediatricians urged toilet training by six months old or that a shot of whisky in a bottle was the cure-all of the day – to know that babies are still wonderfully uncharted territory.

It took me a good six months of 3am Googling and very nearly sending myself mad before it really clicked. All of these sleep solutions work on the presumption that that your baby does not have a personality, that their behaviour can be moulded into the pages of a book. But your baby's personality was decided long before you bought that book and circled it with your silly purple pen. My son, Miller, kicked all night long in the womb from twenty weeks. When he was born he watched every person who came into the hospital room with the kind of suspicious fascination that suggests he will work for MI6 in the future. The world is an exciting assault of new experiences for him, and he has no intention of missing a single one. It should not have come as a surprise to me that my beautiful, curious boy is not a sleeper. Nor should it have surprised me that the advice of an 'expert' would never override the emotions of a mum who wants to help her son stop crying. But it did.

I can't tell you how to make your baby sleep. I can offer no miracle 'cure' because I really believe that this is one thing in your life that you cannot control. But I can tell you that you are most certainly not alone and that somewhere out there – most likely in Islington, the house with the pale blue door – there is a baby who sleeps worse than yours. And that one day your baby *will* 'sleep through', and it will feel like more of an achievement than any medal, promotion or accolade. But until then, here are a few things to circle at 3am that I hope might make you feel a bit better.

You either get a sleeper or you don't

You are not a bad mum if your baby doesn't sleep. I repeat – you are not a bad mum if your baby doesn't sleep. I really thought I was. My neighbour – who is French, incidentally – had a baby three weeks before us. That baby slept for twelve hours a night from ten weeks old. I could see into their lounge from my son's nursery and as I danced around with my microwave dinner stone cold downstairs, having not spoken a civil sentence to my husband for weeks, they were enjoying a home-cooked meal for two. With *candles*.

With the clarity of hindsight and more than two hours of sleep a night, I can see that there is nothing I could have done in those first months to create such a gulf between our babies' sleeping habits. They simply had a sleeper. Some people get sleepers, some do not. Some babies, like people, love routines. Some babies, like people, are spontaneous and excitable and inquisitive. There is no superior parenting here, just different children.

One size does not fit all

You have not made a terrible mistake if you bring your baby into your bed. You are not creating a rod for your own back if you rock your baby to sleep. You are not irresponsible if you co-sleep, or evil if you let your baby cry. A dummy, boob or teddy is not a dangerous prop that will ruin them for life. So tune out the warnings and do what works for you and your baby today.

Don't play the numbers game

I still can't help myself. I've given up with normal social greetings and want to cut straight to the chase – how many hours does your baby sleep? And what about naps, how many? Are they in the cot? Does your baby self soothe? I take on a slightly manic glare as I scattergun my questions at every parent I meet. But it's an ugly habit and I promise you it rarely makes you feel better. So take every day and every night as it comes and remember, motherhood is one place you don't want to play the comparison game.

Sleep training does work (to an extent)

It does. Exhausted and broken by month eight, I tried it. The next night my little boy slept for twelve hours straight. He did the next night, and the next. I started to *believe*. But a few days later he got a cold and the miracle puffed away. Just like losing twelve pounds in twelve days or a no-strings-attached loan, there is *always* a catch. So don't feel pressured into trying a magic solution put forth by any knowing friend or mother-in-law. Don't think that if you *just* stick to the pages of that book it'll all fall into place. Because what works today might not work tomorrow (something it took me a while to realise!) Stick to a rough routine, try not to feed *every* time they cry and don't worry if they cry a little bit, they'll be OK. But most of all, try to keep your sense of humour.

Pick your friends wisely

This is not a time to be loyal. If you happen to have a friend who has a sleeper, I would strongly suggest losing their number for a while. Instead, search for the woman with the same desperate haunted eyes as you. I was lucky enough that this person happened to be one of my very best friends. United in sleep deprivation, we kept each other company at 3am and then faced the world with our eye bags together the next day.

Don't obsess

From some limited Google-based research I can confirm that no one ever died from lack of sleep. So try to stop obsessing about how much you're not getting and see the positives. For example, my son has the most beautiful eyes I've ever seen. Honestly, people stop and stare. And I'm lucky that I get to stare at them all day, and most of the night too ...

1 That you can walk nine miles up a very steep hill, scrub every floor in your house, bounce and bounce and bounce on an exercise ball and eat seven raw chillies

in a row but you cannot, I repeat CANNOT, induce your own labour.

2 That you will feel resentful every single time your partner leaves the house after the birth, and you may well consider various scenarios where you accidentally kill them by banging them over the head with a steriliser. But you will like them again eventually, and, having come out the other side, you'll know that now you're a family.

3 You might find yourself internally repeating 'This is really *hard*' over and over.

4 You will have absolutely no problem picking someone else's nose.

5 Baby TV is a thing. And it's a wondrous, wondrous thing at that.

6 Never trust anyone who tells you to sleep when your baby sleeps. They have clearly never had children. Or they're stupid.

7 You will develop *mumceps* – the kind of fantastically toned, sculpted arms you normally see on Victoria's Secret models. The rest of your skin will look like saggy grey crêpe paper.

8 Never, EVER, feel smug, because the next day it will undoubtedly come back to bite you.

9 Your one and only goal in life will be getting someone else to sleep while you do everything you can to stay awake.

10 Parents lie. And they forget. So be suspicious when they talk of mythical babies who sleep in until 10am or crave broccoli – that baby was awake six times in the night and the broccoli was dipped in Nutella.

11 You will develop the kind of silly, uncontrollable, all-encompassing obsession with your baby that you once felt for a 90s boy band, the kind where just saying their name makes you giddy. But it might not happen overnight.

Mum. Mother. Mama.

By Shobna Gulati

Shobna Gulati is an actress, writer and dancer who has been in *Coronation Street*, Victoria Wood's *Dinnerladies* and also on *Loose Women*. Her son, Akshay, is twenty.

Despite being a little bit chaotic and hedonistic, until the age of 28 I was pretty much doing everything a good Indian girl should. My career was going well, I was married, and it wouldn't have been unreasonable to assume that children would soon be on the cards. Funnily enough, though, I had never really imagined having a child – I was always the baby of my family, and getting married had been more down to the desire for a partner in crime, rather than for the title of 'wife' or 'mother'. I've always felt uncomfortable with labels like that.

Then, while my sisters and brothers were forging ahead, having babies and building their own families, my marriage broke up. I was emotionally bruised and battered, and my mum was hugely disappointed – divorce just wasn't the done thing in our community. I felt that I'd failed my family and, as is too often the case, I couldn't bring myself to have the honest conversation with my mum that we needed to clear the air.

A few months later I was living on friends' sofas in London, but enjoying my newfound freedom. I had work as a dancer, choreographer, teacher and actress, and the play I was in had just won a *Time Out* award and was about to go on tour. I'd had a short, casual relationship after my marriage ended, but a proper relationship was the furthest thought from my mind – I had too much else to do! So when I found myself sitting in the toilet of my temporary flat, holding my breath as a faint blue line insistently appeared on a pregnancy test, all I could think was: 'Oh crap, I've messed things up again ...'

I didn't know what to do or who to tell. I decided to tell my practical, logical sister first, but she told my mum before I had a chance to. My mum, direct and honest as ever, told me how upset she was, and that my life was about to change forever. But she was also clear and practical, and asked if I was considering an abortion. I knew her feelings on abortion but the fact that she even mentioned that she would support me through it meant so much. Yet even the mention of an abortion made me realise that suddenly I wanted this baby more than I had ever wanted anything. I told her, and she said that she'd be there, for both of us.

From the beginning it was a difficult journey – having an unexpected baby on the way is one thing, but doing it alone is another. I was a separated, essentially homeless, culturally excommunicated, single mother-to-be. I stayed in London to hide my pregnancy from all my Manchester *auntijis*, and to prevent bringing further shame on the family. It was a difficult time, but walking around Deptford Market I could be out and proud. Away from the prying eyes, I loved my bump, and the way my show costumes widened to fit around it and my expanding boobs. I felt excited at the prospect of new life and change, despite not really knowing what it would actually mean and how it would change my life as I knew it.

I had only met one single mother in my life. She did reiki and was a chanting Buddhist: calm, collected and together – and with her own home. She'd planned her life this way. I was the polar opposite: I had no plans whatsoever. At the eleventh hour, I realised I really needed my mum. Without hesitation, she said I should move up North to live with her. I moved up on a Sunday, and Akshay was born on the Tuesday. I told you I wasn't one for forward planning.

The birth was all blood, sweat and tears. During labour, all I could think of was *pain*. But the second his body came out of mine, the pain was over. There was just HIM. And suddenly I belonged to the 'hood. The 'motherhood', that is – those silvery scars ingrained into my belly, marking me for ever as 'mother'. I cut his umbilical cord and whispered: 'You're on your own, kid.' I didn't mean it cruelly; after nine months inside me, I was setting him free. In that instant our roles were born. I was his carer, teacher, nurturer, and he was my son.

To be perfectly honest, in the early days I was impatient, sad, tired and lonely – although Akshay is twenty now and sometimes I still am! Each day brought an unexpected challenge. I was unrehearsed and ill-equipped. What are you meant to do? From changing a nappy and examining his poo to monitoring every noise and gurgle, I was constantly uncertain. Was I doing it right? How could I know? I felt guilt, too, about being a single mother. When I registered his name I swear I heard the registrar tutting as I wrestled with whether or not to put Akshay's absent father's name on the birth certificate.

Really, at the beginning, the only thing I felt I did well was breastfeeding. It made me feel close to Akshay, and I was lucky that it worked easily for us. He would feed for hours, and I would feel like we were the only two people in the world. The downside of that was exhaustion. Well, that and smelling like stale dairy all the time, my car splattered with baby milk as I rushed up and down the country teaching dance.

Living with my mum was just what I needed – she was the most expert baby whisperer I had ever seen, and when Akshay was born she was immediately drawn to him. I relied on my mum so much in the first few years of Akshay's life that ultimately she became a mother to both of us. As time went by, my relationship with Mum started to heal and become more open. She was in it with me and helped me through every stage. She showed me how to wash him in the sink (I love those photos), how to change his nappy, how to talk to him. And – in spite of me going against all those cultural norms, and in spite of the onlooking eyes of the family and the wider community, and, in a way, in spite of herself – she showed me love in the highest form. She made the ultimate decision to stand by her daughter.

Still, going back home meant following Mum's rules. And part of me felt it meant I had shown myself unable to manage, that I had failed to graduate into self-sufficient adulthood. Mum and I would fight over every detail of Akshay's babyhood: sleeping, feeding, weaning, sniffles, crying, potty training – and I knew that eventually I wanted to change our circumstances and get us a house where we could go it alone. Still, it was Mum's love for me in this time that taught me the meaning of the word 'mother'.

Slowly, I became more confident about looking after my child, gaining knowledge from my mum along the way. Her wisdom coupled with my unrehearsed methods seemed to work just fine. So when did I really become Akshay's mother? It's hard to say. It wasn't exactly love at first sight, as I was too caught up in the terror of my situation. But as I grew to know him, I grew to know me. I realised I liked him, and I liked who I was becoming. I became responsible for him like my mum was for me, and it made me feel better, more complete, more real. Those self-imposed doubts never fully disappeared, but gradually faded enough to see the light. As the baby turned into Akshay, I turned into his mother.

In retrospect, I would have loved to have shared being a mother with a partner, not least for all it brings to the child. At times, and still today, Akshay and I have found ourselves caught in normal parent/child conflicts, and I sometimes think that having another person there would have helped us find our way out. I would have liked to have celebrated all the highs with someone else too, although Grandma is very good at that.

Even now, I still don't think the word 'mother' suits me. I still don't fit into that stereotype in my head. But perhaps I'm missing the point – I *am* a mother, and so a mother can be anything. I didn't really know what being a mother meant until I appreciated my mum's infinite love for me. So there you go: motherhood for me is a capacity for infinite love. When I think of it like that, I don't mind the word so much.

Akshay is now twenty, and he tries my patience and makes me worry as much as he did when he was tiny, but he's OK, and I still like him. And he still calls me his mama – especially when he wants extra cash!

1 Piles.

2 That boy babies wee in your face and laugh! Usually just after you've changed their nappy.

3 That you need an engineering degree – car seats, buggies, breast pumps, baby monitors, cots and child-proof doors (how do you open them?) are all a nightmare.

4 That toddlers really do toddle … (I know, what was I thinking?)

5 That when breastfeeding you look and smell like a dairy cow and milk can just come in at any point without warning.

6 That it's impossible to wear a sari and keep it either on or clean when you have a child.

7 That you stop seeing your vagina or anything to do with your 'downstairs' after you are six months pregnant and you only realise you have one again while you are giving birth.

8 All the answers to the question: 'Why?'

9 That dangly earrings may make you look like an earth mother, but they are not practical.

10 That you lose your fear of spiders and all things creepy-crawly.

Acknowledgements

This book only came together because of the twenty contributors who decided that they wanted to be part of it, so thank you first to them, with special props going to Anna Moore, Cathy Kelly, Anne Marie Scanlon and Christina Hopkinson, each of whom wrote their chapters entirely on spec, when this book was merely an idea and an outline. Huge and heartfelt thanks also to Vicki Harper for the generous opening of her contacts book, to Emily Young for being a brilliant first reader, to Anna Power for persevering until the answer was 'Yes', to everyone at Icon who worked on the book – especially Kate Hewson for positively painstaking editing – and to Kate Shooter for her inspired cover idea. Most importantly, thanks to the gorgeous Tom Shooter, and our equally gorgeous son, Max, without whom I would never have had the idea in the first place.